THE
LITTLE
BOOK
OF
LINCOLNSHIRE

THE
LITTLE
BOOK
OF
LINCOLNSHIRE

LUCY WOOD

ILLUSTRATED BY
DIANNE CLARK

The
History
Press

This book is dedicated to my beloved late grandfather,
Ronald Limb –
my number one fan,
and I his.

First published 2016

The History Press
The Mill, Brimscombe Port
Stroud, Gloucestershire, GL5 2QG
www.thehistorypress.co.uk

British Library Cataloguing in Publication Data.
A catalogue record for this book is available from the British Library.

ISBN 978 0 7509 6361 9

Typesetting and origination by The History Press
Printed and bound in Great Britain by TJ International Ltd

CONTENTS

ABOUT THE AUTHOR

Lucy Wood qualified as a journalist in 1999. She worked at the *Grimsby Telegraph* for fifteen years as a journalist and news editor. She now works in public relations, and is a qualified PR practitioner. A keen local history enthusiast, she lives in Louth, Lincolnshire.

Also by the Author
The Grimsby Book of Days

ACKNOWLEDGEMENTS

Lincolnshire is the second largest county in England. To cover all of its majesty, mystery and more in one book is impossible but I hope this gives a snapshot of where I'm proud to call home.

I firstly pay credit to the plethora of authors who have chronicled the county over the years. The sizeable bibliography you'll find at the end of this book lists only a handful of the tomes written about Lincolnshire, all of which I wholeheartedly recommend.

The Lincolnshire Archives and library service were invaluable too; such vital and necessary services ensuring our past, present and future are documented. Similarly, I have whiled away many pleasurable hours with the British Newspaper Archive; I think I could spend a decade with its wonderful catalogue and still only read a small percentage.

I'd like to thank my family and my publishers, The History Press, for their support, and Mr Lincolnshire himself, renowned journalist Peter Chapman, for kindly writing the Foreword.

Special mention is reserved for Dianne Clark (a proud Grimbarian) and her beautiful illustrations, and thanks finally to readers of *The Little Book of Lincolnshire*. Researching this book provided enough material to write a sequel, so if you're interested in reading more, please visit http://lucywoodauthor.com. You'll also find information about my first book with The History Press, *The Grimsby Book of Days*.

Lucy Wood, 2016

FOREWORD

Of a winter's eve, the Almighty rings down a glorious curtain along the westwards reaches of Lincolnshire. It is an ever-changing marvel.

Lincolnshire people have become familiar to these sunset spectaculars.

But they have never tired of their vast county, vast skies and magnificent seaboard.

They face east, these Yellowbellies, awaiting the dawn 'when morning gilds the skies', grateful for their good fortune.

Their county is a mysterious place of fen and moor, of wold and marsh, a place of infinite variety.

People have said of Lincolnshire that it guards its secrets, that it is a private place.

Truth is that progress has not affected it overmuch. Add to that the incalculable benefit of the Great North Road which skirts it – seemingly to seal it off, making it not a place 'in transit'. The railways came ... but went.

The very late coming of the Industrial Revolution brought only slight modernity. With modest exceptions there were to be no satanic mills and the county stayed locked in its agricultural past.

Untrammelled by change the county survived, the toll bars, post houses and coaching inns remained in situ until modern times.

The only mills were powered by wind, tall, black flour-streaked giants, and they and the steeples of Anglicanism were the markers of time and place.

It comes as no surprise that nonconformity thrived here, that this is Wesley's county and that recusants found space. The blandishments of establishment never doused the independent spirit.

So vast a county never appealed to the aristocracy. Famous families – and grand houses – were ever few and far between. But the squire and the artisan held sway and do so to this day ... with the poacher on a shiny night!

And what of 'this day'?

Lincolnshire is, above all, a welcoming county. No end of people down the centuries have found refuge here. They found a kindred out-of-step awkwardness in this county and those who stayed never regretted it.

From persecution and wars the county provided an embrace ... for the Dutch, for Russian Jews, for homeless Poles ... for the RAF.

These people, Indians, Icelanders, Danes and so on, married here and thrived. Their surnames survive.

And from stone-built Stamford to terraced Scunthorpe, from the Stump at Boston to the spire at Louth, this extraordinary county exerts its pull.

Those who leave, natives all, do so looking over their shoulders and remain, for the rest of their days, in two minds about what they have abandoned. Lincolnshire is to them as a magnet.

The author and I probably will never leave this place in which we 'move and have our being'.

It is home, warts and all, to both of us.

But you are very welcome to explore it and its mysteries, and wrestle with its vagaries.

This book will prove your guide ... and you will need one before the sun sets in majesty over these shining acres.

Peter Chapman
Journalist and Writer

1

LINCOLNSHIRE LIFE

RELIGIOUS POISONING! OR WAS IT INDIGESTION?

In August 1887, Louth hosted the United Methodist Free Church conference, where about 120 ministers and lay representatives began to suffer the symptoms of poisoning.

The police and doctors were immediately summoned and poisoning was presumed, but the cause was tracked down to their meal, which had contained fermented green peas.

Meanwhile, dodgy tummies galore tainted harvest time in Brigg in August 1859.

There was a widespread bout of chronic diarrhoea among all of the labourers. Men and women, crippled by the urge to go, had to relieve themselves in hedgerows!

A MYSTERIOUS RAILWAY DISASTER

One of the worst railway disasters ever to occur in the county – and one of the greatest mysteries in railway history – happened in Grantham.

On 19 September 1906, the 8.45 p.m. train from London Kings Cross to Edinburgh Waverley departed, made up of coaches, sleepers, mail and parcel vans.

It stopped at Peterborough as scheduled, with a crew and engine change, and left on time towards Grantham, where it was due at 11 p.m.

The points north of Grantham were set onto the sharply curved Nottingham line to accommodate a goods train, while the signals south were set at caution, and the signalman at Grantham North had his lights at danger. All was as it should have been.

That was, until passengers, postmen and railway staff waiting on the platform noticed the train was heading towards them at 50mph – apparently with no intention of stopping.

It whizzed through the station towards the Nottingham line, hit the points and lurched. The locomotive's tender came off the track, dragging the carriages with it. Some carriages slid down an embankment while the rest were tangled on the line.

Fourteen people, including the fireman and driver, were killed. An inquiry was unable to establish whether the brakes had been applied, never mind a cause.

To this day, the tragedy remains an unsolved mystery.

WHO WAS SPRING-HEELED JACK?

Spring-Heeled Jack, the terrifying sensation of Victorian London, made an appearance in Lincolnshire.

Rumours began circulating in the south of the county that a creature, wearing animal skin and springs on his shoes, was seen jumping out of the darkness – petrifying passers-by – and leaping over small buildings and rooftops.

On 3 November 1877, the *Illustrated Police News* quoted a stringer (a rope, twine or cord-maker) from Lincoln, who said the creature could jump up to 20ft. 'Jack' even launched himself through a college window and terrified the ladies inside.

Groups formed to carry out night-time patrols. Two men shot at him as he leapt up Newport Arch, but the skin he was wearing somehow deflected the bullets.

Sightings of Jack were reported around the entire country for sixty-seven years. Was he an alien, an insane acrobat, an eccentric marquis, an escaped kangaroo, or a demon? These are just some of the theories put forward. It's a mystery which causes intrigue to this day.

RESTING FAR FROM HOME

The death of a teenager from Lincolnshire is marked on a headstone far away in Lindisfarne Priory.

The boy, 13-year-old Field Flowers, was on board the steamship *Pegasus* on the night of 19 July 1843, which was undertaking its regular voyage from Leith to Hull.

He was with his sister, 11-year-old Fanny Maria, children of the Reverend Field Flowers, vicar of Tealby in Lincolnshire, and were among fifty-five people on board, including a crew of fourteen.

Six hours after embarking on its voyage, the *Pegasus* struck the Goldstone Rock and sank close to the Farne Islands. The steamer took just forty minutes to sink, and only two passengers and four crew members could be saved.

Field and his sister perished in the tragedy. The siblings had been attending Miss Banks' Boarding School in Edinburgh and were coming home for the holidays in the charge of Miss Maria Barton, the daughter of medical practitioner Zephaniah Barton, from Market Rasen. She too lost her life, as did 27-year-old Robinson Torry, also from Rasen, who had been 'taking a trip for the benefit of his health'.

Miss Barton's body was recovered and received into the family vault the following month. Master Field's body was found by French fishermen, who brought it to Lindisfarne about four weeks after the sinking. His sister's body was never recovered.

THE COUNTY VILLAGE AND THE MATTERHORN

Adorning the church at Skillington are two windows commemorating the Matterhorn disaster of 1865.

Skilled oarsman Charles Hudson was ordained deacon in 1853 and priest the following year, becoming vicar of Skillington in 1860. He was a founder member and secretary of The Alpine Club. By the 1860s, the Matterhorn was the only major unconquered mountain.

Hudson – by now regarded as one of the world's most accomplished mountaineers, who once walked 86 miles in twenty-four hours – was planning to make an attempt on the Matterhorn with 19-year-old Douglas Hadow and Swiss guide Michel Croz, and joined forces in 1865 with another group planning to do the same.

The party began their ascent on 14 July 1865, reaching the summit shortly after midday. While descending, Hadow slipped and fell onto Croz. The climbers were roped together and the impact knocked Hadow and Croz 4,000ft over a ridge, together with Hudson and another climber, Lord Francis Douglas.

Hudson, Hadow and Croz were buried at Zermatt. Lord Douglas's body was never found.

BRITAIN'S WORST INDUSTRIAL EXPLOSION

Flixborough is a small village north of Scunthorpe. On 1 June 1974, it was the location of Britain's worst ever industrial explosion. It had been home to chemical works since 1937, and in 1964, Nypro UK built a plant. Nypro UK was the country's only producer of caprolactam, the main ingredient in the manufacture of nylon. There was a leak in a temporary pipe carrying cyclohexane and the air was filled with a vapour that ignited. The explosion was heard up to 30 miles away, spreading a chemical cloud over Lincolnshire. Twenty-eight people on the site died and more than 100 people – employees and local residents – were injured by flying glass. Every house in the nearby village was damaged and residents were evacuated due to the threat from poisonous fumes. Fire burned on the site for sixteen days following the explosion. Today the site houses an industrial estate.

RAILWAY TRAGEDIES

In 1922, Lincoln's Boultham Chapel was the location of one of the city's largest ever funerals.

On 11 May that year, four local young men – Thomas Pyrah (25), Fred Wheatley (23), Leonard Abell (19) and Arthur Briggs (17) – went out on a ratting trip. On the way home to Boultham, they approached the unmanned pedestrian railway crossing at Coulson Road. A noisy goods train passed, and none of them heard the approach of a passenger train from Nottingham. Their bodies were found a short time later by a passer-by.

Thousands of people lined the streets for their funeral, on 15 May, and the four friends were buried side by side.

Great Northern opened Utterby Halt on the line between Louth and Grimsby on 11 December 1905. It had a small waiting room, two short platforms and a crossing keeper's house, and closed on 11 September 1961. Railway worker John Lancaster set off on a foggy January morning in 1953 to Ludborough Station, walking on the line due to the weather. Near Utterby Halt, he heard a train approaching from behind so stepped onto the adjacent track. The noise drowned out the sound of the approaching Cleethorpes to London train, and he was killed.

In December 1932 a shocking discovery was made on the LNER railway line near the Welholme Road crossing in Grimsby.

The decapitated body of a man was found by the guard of a goods train. He was later identified as a retired builder.

It was customary for such trains to stop at the crossing, and it was during this halt that the guard, Mr Flint, came upon the man's severed head in a nearby six-foot. Other parts of his body were found elsewhere.

It was discovered that the deceased had tragically been struck by the onward-bound mail train, which arrived in Grimsby at 5.22 a.m. each day.

Tragedy struck at Melton Ross railway bridge in 1879. The structure had been unstable for some time and work began on its demolition and reconstruction.

Scaffolding was put in place in seventeen spots along the bridge to support explosives, but some failed to detonate and the workmen began taking down the bridge manually, despite the obvious danger.

At 3.30 a.m. on 3 February, an arch where more than a dozen men were working by oil lamp collapsed.

The rescue operation took seven hours. Ellis Hornsby, Edward Ambler and Thomas Robinson lost their lives, twelve of their colleagues were badly hurt and others suffered minor injuries.

A MOST DARING SEA RESCUE

An incident of endurance played out in complete darkness – and in the middle of a snow blizzard – on 12 February 1940.

Grimsby trawler *Gurth* found herself in trouble, and called on RNLI coxswain Robert Cross for help.

Two of the lifeboat crew were ill when they were called out to the *Gurth*, so it was manned by only six in total, and Cross couldn't spare anyone to operate the searchlight. The rescuers were repeatedly knocked down by the sea and were only saved from being washed overboard by hanging on to the handrails. A rope which had washed overboard became tangled around the propeller and for some time only one engine on the lifeboat functioned.

Three-and-half hours later, the entire crew of the *Gurth* were safe on shore, albeit bruised and battered, and eternally thankful to Cross and his shattered men.

Cross won the RNLI gold medal for gallantry and the George Medal for the *Gurth*'s rescue, and his five-man crew each won the silver medal. He held the post of coxswain for thirty-one years, retiring in 1943 aged 67, and lived to the age of 88, having taken part in the rescue of 453 lives.

THE MURDEROUS MONKEY

In 1730 Sir Michael Newton, the owner of Culverthorpe Hall near Sleaford, married Margaret and they had a son. The family's pet monkey climbed into the newborn's cot while at their London home and carried the child to a balcony, throwing him onto the flagstones below and bringing to an end the male line of the Newton family. Lady Margaret hid her distress by being outwardly sociable, attending gatherings in expensive trademark blue clothes. Culverthorpe Hall is said to be haunted by a Blue Lady.

THE MAN WHO OFFICIALLY DIDN'T EXIST

In April 1932, Tom Lapidge, a mate on the *Capricornus*, vanished… or did he?

The *Capricornus* was heading home and the crew had turned in for the night. Lapidge was alone with the compass and at 4 a.m. he called for a cup of tea.

A deckhand went to the bridge – but there was no one there. Only Lapidge's belt, sou'wester, oilfrock and his pipe remained. The deckhand roused the skipper and crew, and the ship was searched. They re-traced their path for 4 miles but nothing was found, so they headed for Grimsby.

An inquiry concluded Lapidge, from Healing, had been washed overboard and that was the end of the matter… until August, when he emerged – alive and well – at his daughter-in-law's home.

'He claimed that, officially, he didn't exist,' recalled a fellow fisherman. 'He devised a plan to defraud an insurance company by faking his death. He hid away in the ship's bunkers. When the ship docked, he sneaked ashore under cover of darkness and made his way to Hull, where he had arranged to meet his wife. He told me his wife duly drew the insurance – but instead of joining him, she made off with another man!'

A SCANDALOUS COUNTY

Passionate letters left in a hedge, a seduction followed by abandonment and a tragic pregnancy… it's the stuff novels are made of, but happened in Lincolnshire more than 100 years ago.

When solicitor Sidney Bazalgette Carnley, of Norbury House, Alford, married Ellen in 1884, little did the couple know that Ellen would soon become an invalid. This unhappy state led to Sidney becoming friendly with Miss Florence Wilson, the daughter of the clerk to the Alford Justices, who resided in Bleak House, the adjoining property. By 1894, Ellen was completely bedridden and Sidney's relationship with Florence developed to the point that Sidney promised to marry her as soon as he was free of his wife.

Sidney wrote love letters to Florence, leaving them in the hedge between the properties, but it was not until 1900 that he seduced the young miss – and immediately rejected her. Florence, now pregnant, fled from Alford to Southwell and then Wimbledon, where the child was born but survived for less than a week.

When she returned to Alford, Sidney declared his love for Florence, and although she spurned him at first, she tried to repair their friendship when she became worried about financial matters.

In January 1906 Ellen died and by now Sidney was not interested in Florence. Florence, however, had other ideas. She wrote to her former beau demanding marriage, threatening to expose his dishonour. She followed him around Alford, arranged to have photographs taken of him with other women and had the images printed on postcards with insulting messages attached. Obscene messages were scrawled with chalk on the walls and doors of Norbury House.

Eventually the argument went to court. Florence successfully sued for breach of promise, and Sidney's defence that his promise of marriage was not legal as he was still wed at the time was also upheld. The result was that Florence was awarded £100 in damages and Sidney a farthing for being libelled.

Because of Sidney's wealth, rumours about his personal conduct did little to affect his social standing. He became a prominent townsman in Alford and bred horses until about 1930. He died in 1947.

From modest beginnings, Ernest Terah Hooley became a famous English millionaire, at stages in his life owning stately homes Sudbrooke Holme and Temple Belwood, as well as making an attempt to purchase Tattersall Castle.

But it was the revelation that he was a swindler which brought him to notoriety.

He had the outward appearance of having keen financial skills, and was certainly able to spot opportunities before anyone else. For example, realising that cycling was becoming popular in 1894, he swiftly floated the Swift, Singer and Raleigh manufacturing firms. He also purchased Dunlop Pneumatic Tyre Company – one of his biggest coups.

But Hooley was declared bankrupt in 1897 and an expected knighthood and parliamentary candidature were withdrawn.

Two years along, while still an undischarged bankrupt, he purchased a concession from the Tsar of Russia to exploit Siberian goldfields. He paid £75,000 and sold it to a public company for £1 million – just one example of his entrepreneurial skills.

However, in 1904 Hooley was tried at the Old Bailey for conspiring to defraud a publican called Paine, who had invested £27,000 in the Siberian goldfields and received a piece of gold-bearing quartz in return. Hooley and his co-defendant, financier Henry John Lawson, were acquitted.

He spent time buying country estates and splitting up the land to sell on. Skip to 1912 and Hooley was again before the Old Bailey, this time on a charge of false pretences relating to the sale of a Nottinghamshire estate. This time he was jailed for twelve months, and when released led a quiet life until he was tempted to dabble in the rise of the Lancashire cotton industry.

In 1920, he was charged with conspiracy to commit fraud in connection with the purchase of shares of a cotton mill. The five-week trial, in which Hooley was branded as the swindling ringleader, saw him jailed for three years.

Following his release he lived in Derbyshire, making a living mainly by selling pigs. In 1939, aged 80, he was again made bankrupt. He died in a guesthouse aged 88 in 1947.

In 1923, a high society affair was revealed. Australian journalist Eugenia Stone, a 6ft 2in beauty of 28, swept widowed Sir George Doughty, Grimsby's MP, off his feet.

She wed Sir George (53), who owned the *Grimsby Evening Telegraph*, and wrote a column in it, under her own name – in a high moral tone – on many subjects. But another side to Lady Doughty was revealed.

Following Sir George's death in 1914, she left Grimsby for London, and was a frequent visitor to the Riviera.

Sir George's great friend, T.G. Tickler, became infatuated with her, despite being married with four children, and by 1920 he was living half with his wife and half with Lady Doughty. He told his wife if she didn't like it, she could leave. In 1923, Mrs Tickler discovered a bundle of erotic letters written to her husband, and decided to divorce him.

When the court was told Tickler had broken into his wife's bedroom brandishing a loaded pistol and threatened to kill her and himself, the tone of the affair was confirmed.

The divorce was granted. Tickler never married Lady Doughty nor returned to Grimsby – he eventually re-married in 1955, to a Mrs Brown, whom he had known for thirty-three years.

LINCOLN'S LOST RAILWAY STATION

St Mark's was the city's first station and opened on 3 August 1846, with direct routes to London. It closed on 13 May 1985, making Lincoln's central station the one and only for citizens.

To mark the closure Dr Philip Marshal, then Lincoln Cathedral's organist, set to music an inscription from a memorial in Ely Cathedral. The memorial was to two railwaymen who died in an accident in 1845. The city cathedral's choir sang the composition on the platform at the central station.

St Mark's was marred by an accident of its own, when a small cannon in the station grounds burst during celebrations on the official opening day. Mr Paul Harding was struck by a piece of metal, forcing his leg to be amputated, and a boy was struck on the hand, causing the loss of two fingers.

DIVING PROFESSORS IN SKEGNESS

In days gone by, tourists would flock to the Lincolnshire coast to take in the attractions on offer.

In Skegness, a 90ft diving stage was constructed where divers – known as professors – would show off their sporting prowess. One of the earliest was Professor Capes, of Hull, followed by Professor Connell in the 1890s.

In 1904, Professor Leo Cranford, of Brooklyn Bridge – known for his feats in the US – travelled to the resort to thrill the crowds by riding a bicycle off a 70ft platform into the briny.

In the 1920s and '30s, one-legged Professor F.C. Gadsby and his son, Dare Devil Leslie, attracted the attention of *Daily Mirror* columnist Maurice Lane-Norcott. Of the senior Gadsby, he wrote: 'I can't understand why the angels have never fetched him away long ago; he is always up to mischief. His latest amusement is to set himself on fire and jump off the Pier into a blazing furnace 4'9" deep. His is a busy life.'

Of Skegness itself, he wrote: 'It is easily like a piece of Margate, and a slice of Ostend, and a little bit of Wembley and a morsel of the Lido, the whole being nicely flavoured with girlish sauce and well-baked in sunshine!'

In later years, Dare Devil Leslie played a major role in several sea dramas, coming to the rescue of tourists in distress.

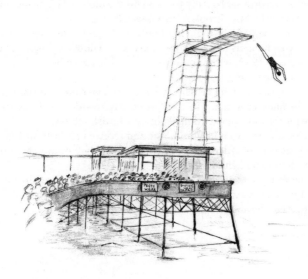

HANDLE WITH CARE

In June 1854, porters on the Manchester, Sheffield and Lincolnshire Railway at Grimsby were transferring property and goods from a London train when they found a package marked 'Glass, with care'.

It was addressed to a reverend in a nearby village, but they thought the package looked suspicious and opened it. Inside they discovered the body of the reverend's daughter. It was duly repackaged and sent to the gentleman, but with an extra bill for carrying a corpse.

It had been sent at a cost of £1 4s, when it should have been £8.

ONE OF THE FINEST AVIATION ACHIEVEMENTS

World record breaker Alex Henshaw's education at Lincoln School from 1922 to 1927 inducts him into the Lincolnshire hall of fame.

While in Lincolnshire, his father, Albert, established one of the first holiday camps in the country, at the Trusville Holiday Estate near Mablethorpe, and aged 12, Alex was awarded a Royal Life-Saving Medal for saving a boy from drowning in the River Witham.

But it is for his airborne antics that Alex is remembered. He flew in a Mew Gull G-AEXF from Gravesend, Kent, to Cape Town and back – breaking all world records for solo or multi-crew flights.

He broke records set by Amy Johnson for the outward flight and the return journey by H.L. Brook by fifty-seven hours.

Alex's outbound flight took 392 hours over 6,300 miles. He rested for twenty-eight hours in Cape Town and touched down on English soil on 9 February 1939, with just eleven minutes between his outbound and inward flight times.

This remarkable achievement is hailed by aviation historians as one of the finest ever made. In 1940, Alex was awarded the Britannia Trophy for the most outstanding flight by a British subject.

He served in the Second World War and received an MBE in 1945. In 1995, he was awarded a Spitfire Trophy on behalf of the Battle of Britain Memorial Flight.

Incidentally, his son maintained connections with Lincolnshire by operating farms at Theddlethorpe, Mablethorpe, Sutton-on-Sea, Huttoft, Anderby and Chapel St Leonards.

THE LINCOLNSHIRE RISING

In 1536, some Lincolnshire folk were outraged that King Henry VIII planned to dissolve minor monasteries and raise taxes. They rebelled and this became known as the Lincolnshire Rising. Thomas Foster was a chairman in Louth, and one Sunday evening in 1536 sparked the rebellion by shouting as the vicar of Louth finished his sermon. His outburst caused turmoil and by the next day, Louth had declared itself openly against the government of Henry VIII, though not against the King himself.

The movement swept through the county; thousands of men began marching to London and for a short time, the monarchy was under threat.

The rising began in October of that year in Louth, Horncastle and Caistor, from where people marched to Lincoln. Feelings were so high that Dr Raynes, Chancellor of Louth, was dragged to Horncastle by a mob and clubbed to death.

A letter was sent to the King about their grievances, prompting the King to slate the county as 'one of the most brute and beastly in the realm'.

A number of rebels were hanged. Thirty-six of the fifty-two monasteries in Lincolnshire were dissolved by August 1536.

THE LION'S MAKEOVER

A prank famous in Lincoln lore took place at The Arboretum in May 1909.

The Arboretum Lion was a life-size stone statue in the grounds of the pleasure garden, on a plinth 18ft high.

It had been presented in 1872 by the Mayor, Francis Clarke, who became wealthy through sales of his 'Blood Mixture' – a purifying tonic which claimed to cure diseases caused by blood impurities. Under cover of darkness, a gang gathered at The Arboretum, out-witted the superintendent and gave the lion a makeover. The statue's feet and head were painted with red primer, its tail daubed in black and its body in yellow and red stripes.

The culprits were never caught but rumours spread. The *Lincoln Leader* reported it could have been 'the work of some aggrieved representative of the unemployed or someone who had a spite against the Corporation. We have even heard the suggestion that German invaders have perpetrated the abuse as an "insult" to the British Lion.'

Critch's Annual of 1909 published this ditty to mark the joke:

> The prank was played at midnight,
> When the pubs and clubs were closed.
> And 'cos the lion couldn't bite,
> The deed was bravely posed.

2

PLACES AND LANDMARKS

A KINKY ROMAN ROAD

Roman roads are straight, and Ermine Street – running from Lincoln to the Humber – is no exception. Or is it? The Scampton kink is the only bend in the street's route, and the cause was the Second World War. Brattleby Airfield opened in 1916 but closed in 1919. It was rebuilt in 1939 as its more famous incarnation, RAF Scampton, a base for Bomber Command. Vulcan bombers required a single 9,000ft runway, hence the Scampton kink was created.

ONE OF MANY DESERTED VILLAGES

Remains of the deserted village of Riseholme are visible today if you look hard. Believed to be of Saxon origin, the village was also home to Riseholme Hall, built in the late eighteenth century by the Chaplain family. It became the official residence for the Bishops of Lincoln from 1840 until 1887, when the estate was sold to Captain Wilson. Fast-forward to 1946 and it was sold to Lindsey County Council, which established an agricultural college. The estate also includes Caythorpe Court, which was built in 1903 for Edgar Lubbock.

TEN FAMILIAR LANDMARKS

One of the best-known sea marks of the Humber is the 309ft Dock Tower at Grimsby – taller than Lincoln Cathedral and made with about a million bricks. It was designed by J.W. Wild, who travelled widely in Egypt, Syria and southern Europe, gathering sketches of ideas, some of which he used in Grimsby. At its construction, it was the highest brick building in the country; its cast-iron spiral staircase of 350 steps is the longest in the world. Although it looks ornamental, it was built as part of the hydraulic lock gates system. About 247ft up is a 30,000-gallon capacity water tank. It was later used for washing down the fish markets and firefighting. On the north-west face is a plaque commemorating the men of the minesweepers who lost their lives in the Second World War. Unveiled in 1948, it is the only tribute of its kind to the minesweeping service, of which Grimsby was one of the largest bases.

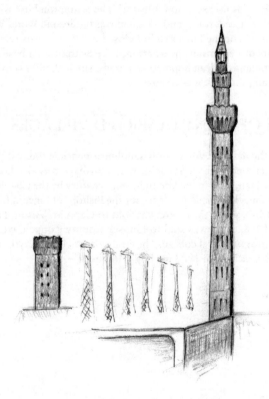

The Humber Bridge was opened by the Queen on 17 July 1981, with a world record-breaking total length of 2,220m, and a centre span of 1,410m. It lost the record seventeen years later to a bridge in Japan, which centrally spanned 1,990m. With one part in Lincolnshire and the other in Yorkshire, the bridge spans two counties. The cables supporting the road are made of 14,948 strands of galvanised wire.

Old Clee Church, Grimsby's oldest building, was dedicated on 5 March 1192 by St Hugh, the first Bishop of Lincoln, during the reign of Richard the Lionheart. The Saxon tower dates back to around 1050. The nave was rebuilt and the transepts added in Norman times.

Immingham Dock is among a handful of Britain's ports built in the twentieth century. The Great Central Railway Company embarked on constructing the King's Dock in 1906. It was officially opened by King George V seven years later.

Scunthorpe's steelworks are a familiar sight, and its origins are thanks to the Romans, who used the ironstone deposits in the land there. Skip to 1864 and the Frodingham Iron Company came along. In 1890, steel production began. The site has four furnaces, named Queen Mary, Queen Victoria, Queen Anne and Queen Bess.

Grimsthorpe Castle was given to the Willoughby de Eresby family by Henry VIII in 1516 as a wedding gift, when the 10th Lord married Maria de Salinas, Katherine of Aragon's cousin. The family built an extension when Henry VIII announced he was coming to stay.

Waltham Windmill has been blown down twice. The mill was built in 1666 and devastated by a storm in 1744, so it was replaced but destroyed again in a gale in 1873, and again replaced. During the Second World War, it was made sail-less so it posed no threat to aircraft from Waltham Airfield.

Skegness Pier, described as the finest in England, officially opened in June 1881. It was 1,843ft long and 24ft wide, and the fourth longest pier in England. It was constructed by Skegness Pier Company for £22,000 by the 9th Earl of Scarborough, who was credited for transforming Skegness into a holiday resort. A popular ditty, the Skegness Polka, was written by Henry Houseley in 1882 and dedicated to the earl's wife. It was followed in 1897 by the Skegness Waltz, written by Carl Schynor and dedicated to the 10th Earl.

Gainsborough Old Hall was built by the Burgh family in about 1460 and then sold to the Hickmans. Famous visitors included Richard III, Henry VIII, John Wesley and the Pilgrim Fathers.

Thornton Abbey, in North Lincolnshire, is among only a handful of British abbeys that survived Henry VIII's Dissolution of the Monasteries. It escaped by becoming a secular college until it closed in 1547. Its gatehouse is the largest in England.

UNDERGROUND:
ARCHAEOLOGICAL DISCOVERIES

A Roman villa was discovered in 1818 by workmen widening a road at Haceby. It was partially excavated by the RAF College at Cranwell during 1928 and 1929 and the remains of several rooms were uncovered, including the hot room of a bathhouse. Historians believe the villa was occupied from the second to the fourth century AD.

The Sudbrook Torc was found in 1922 by Royce Marshal while harrowing a field at Sudbrook, near Ancaster. He found a gold neck ring (torc), a symbol of power and wealth during the Bronze Age. The discovery was one of only seven examples of its type, and the first to be found in Britain.

Hearths and pottery used during salt-making were discovered during an excavation of a Roman village near Holbeach. Evidence of a hut and rubbish dump, containing broken pottery, were found.

The remains of a Roman house with underfloor heating was discovered west of Lincoln Cathedral, near to the Exchequer Gate, while a cellar was being constructed in 1739.

One of the finest examples of an Iron-Age shield in Europe was found in Lincolnshire. The Witham Shield was dredged from the River Witham, near Lincoln, in 1826. It's on permanent display in the British Museum.

5,700 silver pennies from Henry II's reign, minted between 1154 and 1180 at twenty-eight different mints, were uncovered by a ploughman near Caistor High Street in 1807. The coins were buried in an earthenware vessel, and became known as the Tealby Hoarde. More than 5,000 of the coins were melted by the Royal Mint but some remained at the British Museum.

In 1959 the Walesby Tank, a Roman font possibly used for baptisms, was ploughed up near the site of a Roman villa. It is one of the most important relics of early Christianity in Britain.

THE OLDEST EVER INN?

Lincolnshire's oldest coaching inn, and possibly the oldest in the country, is thought to be Grantham's Angel and Royal. It stands on what was the Great North Road and was built about 600 years ago.

Seven kings of England and other members of the royal family have stayed there, including George IV and Richard III.

It was known as The Angel until 1866, when the Prince of Wales paid a visit. It was agreed that the visit should be marked, so Royal was added to the inn's name.

TEN LOST COUNTRY HOUSES

Uffington House, Stamford, belonged to the Bertie family from 1673 and was destroyed by fire in 1904.

The last inhabitant of Thonock Hall, Gainsborough, was eccentric bachelor Sir Hickman Beckett Bacon, the 11th and 12th Baronet. He was so shocked at the price of coffins that he bought his own for 35s. The house was closed up after his death in 1945 and demolished in 1964; it had no gas, electricity or bathrooms.

Syston Hall, South Kesteven, was the main seat of the Thorold family, who owned many houses throughout Lincolnshire. In 1823, a blaze broke out in the library. The house was uninhabited after 1912, apart from during the war years when it was home to temporary tenants. The hall was famous for its huge library of rare books, including a copy of the Gutenburg Bible. Its contents were sold in 1922 and the hall demolished in 1928.

Walmsgate Hall, Burwell, was owned by Captain Thomas Yorke Dallas Yorke, of the 11th Hussars, who was almost 7ft tall. Field master of the Southwold Hunt, he was introduced to Napoleon III as the most handsome officer in the British Army. He died in 1924, two years shy of his 100th birthday. The captain's only daughter, Winifred, married the 6th Duke of Portland and became a famous hostess. The hall was left to his second grandson, and sold to the Haggas family before being demolished in the 1950s.

Haverholme Priory, Sleaford, was originally a monastic site and later in the Finch Hatton family. One incumbent, Murray Finch Hatton, the 12th Earl of Winchelsea, was MP for Lincolnshire South between 1844 and 1887. He kept a pet lion, which would rest on the drawing room sofa. He later gave it to London Zoo.

Stourton Hall, near Baumber, was inhabited by the Livesey family. Joseph Montague Livesey, who died in 1902, was an innovator. At his design, gas used in the glass houses on the 307-acre estate came from chicken manure and he also had a steam yacht on the lake. The hall passed to his reclusive son, Algernon, who died in 1951. It was sold two years later to a timber importer, and demolished.

Elkington Hall, South Elkington, was home of the Smyth family, and built in 1842. The last of the Smyths, William Grenville, rode a bicycle 600 miles from John O'Groats to Louth in sixty hours without assistance. William broke many road-racing records as an amateur. The estate was sold in the 1930s and remained unoccupied until its demolition in the 1960s.

In 1879, Denton Manor, Grantham, belonged to the Welby family, whose connection to the building dates to 1523. In January 1906, the manor was damaged by a fire sparked in the private chapel, probably caused by a flue overheating. A housemaid saw the skirting boards were alight and raised the alarm. The house survived but was demolished in the late 1930s.

Manby Hall, between Broughton and Ashby, belonged to the Anderson family. A unique feature was an engraved pane of glass, which read: 'Nine ladies dined with ye widower, Jan ye 12th, 1743.' The hall was sold in 1949, through death duties, and bought by the 2nd Duke of Westminster for shooting, but it was mostly in ruins.

West Willoughby Hall, between Sleaford and Grantham, was built in 1876 by William Watkins. It was said Frederick Allix had it constructed in a Flemish style to tempt his wife, who lived in Belgium, to move to Lincolnshire. She never did. It was empty throughout the 1930s and badly treated by the Army during the Second World War. On 4 November 1964 it was demolished – the anniversary of the death of its last resident, Harold Hitchcock, who had died in 1941.

A MISCELLANY OF FACTS

Did you know that a major Cleethorpes landowner was a Cambridge institution? Sidney Sussex College created the regimented township of New Cleethorpes. It donated 12 acres to the council to create Sidney Park.

Grimsby Town FC's home is actually in Cleethorpes. Blundell Park opened in 1901.

A historical maze survives at Alkborough. First recorded in the seventeenth century, historians believe its origins may lie in the twelfth century when Benedictine monks from Spalding set up a grange nearby.

Stamford, which lies where several prehistoric trackways cross, was built on the site of an ancient geomantic earthwork in the shape of a running bull. In 1989, historians and archaeologists discovered that the bull runs from east to west across the town. It is known as the Stamford Taurus.

A ferry to Hull was established from New Holland in 1825, and the Manchester, Sheffield and Lincolnshire Railway constructed a pier, dock and village at the end of its line. It became a port for coal, bricks and timber, and ship-breaking yards were established. Ferries *Wingfield Castle*, *Tattershall Castle* and *Lincoln Castle* carried passengers across the river until the Humber Bridge opened in 1981. *Tattershall Castle* now lives on the River Thames in London as an entertainment venue.

Tetney's blow wells are one of the area's finer natural occurrences. For years the fresh water springs were considered bottomless; they were explored by divers in 1961, and found to be only 16ft deep.

Louth owns one of the earliest aerial pictures. In 1844, while repairs were being carried out to the spire of St James' Church, William Brown sketched his panorama from the scaffolding, clearly showing the medieval street plan.

Market Rasen has no high street; instead, it has King Street and Queen Street, with the Market Place separating them. The town was originally called East Rasen and is well known for its racecourse.

A BRIEF HISTORY OF ALFORD

Alford didn't fare well when the plague struck in the 1630s. One hundred deaths were recorded by the town vicar.

A Plague Stone was erected at Miles Cross Hill, where residents would put money in a hollowed-out bowl filled with vinegar, which they used as a disinfectant, to pay the brave townsfolk of Spilsby who would venture out with food to help their needy neighbours.

The town's manor house was built by Sir Robert Christopher in 1660, and a grammar school was founded in 1556. One of its most famous pupils was John Smith, the explorer whose life was saved by Pocahontas.

Smith was born in either 1579 or 1580 and baptised at Willoughby. He joined the French Army and later entered the service of the Archduke of Austria. At the Battle of Rothenthurm he was captured and sold as a slave, but escaped to England in 1605.

In December 1606, he emigrated with 105 others to Virginia. He was a member of the council appointed to administer the colony and was on an expedition for food when he was captured by Native Americans. It was Pocahontas's intervention that saved him.

By 1608 he was head of the colony, but an accidental injury saw him return to England. He died in London in 1631.

STRANGE PLACE NAMES

When in Lea, you may come across a place called Cavendish's Bog.

Its name dates back to 1643, when Royalists were attacked by Cromwell there. Royalist commander General Charles Cavendish was killed by a sword through the ribs as he was trapped in a quagmire.

Ding Dong Wood once existed in West Rasen. It was left to the parish to pay for the ringing of church bell on winter nights, and was destroyed through the Enclosures Act.

Other unusual place names include:

Cold Harbour   Tongue End
Spital-In-The-Street   Muckton Bottom
Mavis Enderby   Wasp's Nest

WHY INGOLDMELLS HAS A PALM TREE

A palm tree stands outside Ingoldmells church. Legend has it that the squire's daughter, Charlotte, fell in love with Jonah, a servant. They would meet secretly at the church, and one time the squire saw them. He severely disapproved of the match and Jonah was sent to sea, where he died in a shipwreck.

His body was returned to Ingoldmells and a palm tree planted to grow over his grave. Poor Charlotte, it is said, died of a broken heart.

THE MARMIONS AND THE DYMOKES

Scrivelsby was home to the Champions of England; the Marmion and the Dymoke families.

It was the Champions' job to attend every coronation and challenge anyone who disputed the monarch's claim on the kingdom to a battle. From the time of Richard II, this duty fell to the Marmions, which was passed through marriage to the Dymokes.

Sir John Dymoke was Champion for the coronation of Lincolnshire's only king, Henry of Bolingbroke.

SOME MONASTIC RUINS

Bardney Abbey: This seventh-century building was destroyed by the Vikings in 1087.

Barlings Abbey: This Premonstratensian abbey was founded in 1154, and implicated in the Lincolnshire Rising of 1536. Its abbot and four canons were executed.

Crowland Abbey: Founded by St Guthlac in the eighth century.

Kirkstead Abbey: Founded by Hugh Brito, Lord of Tattershall, in 1139. It was dissolved in 1537: its last abbot, Richard Harrison, and three of his monks were executed after being implicated in the Lincolnshire Rising.

St Leonard's Priory: A Benedictine priory founded in 1082. Edward I once stayed there.

South Kyme Priory: Founded by Philip of Kyme, steward to the Earl of Lincoln, sometime before 1169. In 1440, Bishop Alnwick visited and reported that the prior complained that his canons were too fond of idle sports.

Tupholme Abbey: Founded between 1155 and 1165. In 1357, an abbot was accused of forging coins. He used the counterfeit cash to buy wine and corn, and sell them on for profit. In 1497, Thomas Pynderwelle was banished from the abbey for fathering the child of a local woman.

STEP BACK IN TIME

Walk into Barkham Street, Wainfleet, and you are transported from rural Lincolnshire to Victorian London.

The smart row of homes was built on land given to London's Bethlehem Hospital – also known as Bedlam – by Sir Edward Barkham.

The houses were designed by architect Sydney Smirke, apparently without consideration of what Lincolnshire is actually like; they are completely, but beautifully, at odds with the rest of the area.

THE 68TH CINEMA TO OPEN IN BRITAIN

If you enjoy going to the cinema, then take a trip to Woodhall Spa.

The Kinema in the Woods was originally a farm building, and is the only remaining cinema in the UK to use rear projection.

In 1906, it was a cricket pavilion for Petwood House, and converted in 1922 by Captain Allport into the Pavilion Cinema. He ran it until 1973, when it was purchased by James Green.

THE DISNEY CONNECTION

Walt Disney had no birth certificate, and what record he could find was dated ten years before he could have been born.

This discrepancy troubled him for many years, so in the late 1940s he travelled to Lincolnshire to investigate his possible roots, in the small village of Norton Disney.

One of William the Conqueror's soldiers, a member of the d'Isigne family, was granted property at Norton and became Lord of the Manor.

The family name was anglicised to Disney and, in 1834, some members emigrated to America.

When Walt visited the village, he was photographed reading church registers and recorded his brief time there in his diary.

NEVER MIND ITALY: LINCOLNSHIRE'S LEANING TOWERS

Skegness Clock Tower leans slightly. The tower and spire of St Lawrence's Church, in Surfleet, leans by about 6ft at the top. In Pinchbeck, St Mary's Church tower at the bottom leans, yet the top is straight. St Peter's Church, at Thorpe St Peter, and St Clement's, in Sutton-on-Sea, both suffer from leaning towers. The west towers of Lincoln Cathedral are wider apart at the top than at the bottom.

3

LINCOLNSHIRE PEOPLE

THE HORNCASTLE EXECUTIONER

William Marwood perfected the technique of hanging known as the 'long drop'.

Born in Goulceby and originally a cobbler, he was 54 when he persuaded the governor of Lincoln Castle Gaol to allow him to conduct an execution.

His efficiency in executing William Frederick Horry on 1 April 1872 saw him appointed public hangman. The 'long drop' ensured that prisoners' necks were broken instantly, and was considered more humane. He initially kept his job a secret, even from his wife, but was proud of his work and displayed rope he used in his workshop in Horncastle.

He was in office from 1874 to 1883, with a retainer of £20 a year plus £10 for each execution. He was allowed to keep felons' clothes and claim travel expenses. His notable cases included burglar and murderer Charles Peace and Irish servant Kate Webster, who murdered her mistress with an axe.

He also executed Joe Brady and four other members of the Invincibles gang for murders in Dublin, including that of Lord Frederick Cavendish and Thomas Harry Burke, Ireland's Permanent Under Secretary at Britain's Irish Office.

Married twice and childless, Marwood died in 1883. His last hanging was two weeks before, in London. Rumours were that he was poisoned in revenge for the Dublin executions, but his death certificate recorded pneumonia, aggravated by liver and kidney disease. His clothes and effects were sold to souvenir hunters; even his tombstone was chipped at by fans wanting a memento.

THE MAN WHO BOUGHT THE LINCOLN IMP

Lincoln philanthropist James Ward Usher left a legacy for the city.

He joined his father's jewellers' and watchmakers' business in 1860, taking sole control fourteen years later and becoming the first city businessman to use electric light.

His business acumen led him to acquire the rights to reproduce the Lincoln Imp in jewellery. The imp is Lincoln Cathedral's famous gargoyle and the official symbol of the city.

He sold hundreds of gold and silver jewellery pieces, some encrusted with diamonds, and is reported to have given a pin to the Prince of Wales.

Mr Usher was also a collector of objets d'art and travelled thousands of miles to amass a vast catalogue. His will, made two days before he died, gifted the collection to the city and left money to build the Usher Gallery.

STRIKING A NOTE: MUSICAL LINCOLNSHIRE

William Byrd was an English composer of the Renaissance, and his first known professional employment was in 1563 as organist and master of the choristers at Lincoln Cathedral. He lived in Minster Yard, was married and fathered at least seven children.

He was in post until 1572, when he became a gentleman of the Chapel Royal and joint organist with Thomas Tallis, but maintained his links with Lincoln; the Dean and Chapter paid a quarter of his salary in return for church songs until 1581.

In 1575, Byrd and Tallis were jointly granted a patent for printing music and ruled music paper for twenty-one years. When Tallis died in 1585, the licence became William's alone.

Byrd made 470 compositions overall.

Sir Neville Mariner was born in 1924 in Lincoln. His father, Herbert, was a music teacher and choral conductor.

Sir Neville studied at the Lincoln School and then the Royal College of Music before teaching at Eton. He was appointed Professor of the Royal College in 1950, Music Director of the Los Angeles Chamber Orchestra between 1968 and 1977, and Director of the Stuttgart Radio Symphony Orchestra from 1984 to 1989. In 1956, he founded the Academy of St Martin in the Fields, and has conducted all major symphony orchestras in the world. He was knighted in 1985.

Australian-born folk song collector Percy Grainger has Lincolnshire to thank for some of his success.

In 1900, he went on a concert tour which brought him to England in 1901. Three years later he performed on piano in Grimsby – his first contact with the county. In 1905, he attended the folk songs class at Brigg's North Lincolnshire Musical Competition and later that year undertook a bike tour of Lincolnshire with George Elwes, a Brigg tenor, to collect examples of folk songs.

'Brigg Fair', 'Seventeen Come Sunday' and 'March to the Battlefield' were among this haul, and were published in time for the 1906 competition.

In July of that year, Percy went to Broughton to note three songs from Thomas Stark. He then went to Brigg, where thirty-one songs were placed onto phonograph.

By 1908, he had completed his collection and created many arrangements, including 'Lincolnshire Posy' for wind-band or two pianos. He died in America in 1961.

Composer and organist John Taverner – regarded as one of the most important English composers of his era – was born in Boston in about 1490.

In 1526, he became a choristers' instructor in Oxford. He was paid £10 a year, given 4 yards of cloth for livery, and 1s 8d a week for food.

During this time, he wrote many religious works. By 1537, he had returned to Boston. In 1545, he became alderman but died and was buried at St Botolph's.

FAMILIES WHO MADE THEIR MARK

The Curtois family had connections with the Branston area for more than 200 years; seven members of the family were parish rectors, and the connection was unbroken from 1680 to 1861, when Reverend Peregrine died.

Algernon Curtois – one of eleven children to Atwill Curtois – was educated at Oxford, ordained in 1894 and became a licensed priest in the Lincoln Diocese in 1901. He was curate of St Mary's Church in Lincoln from 1893 to 1896, and of St Swithins from 1896 to 1901.

Algernon's sisters were also notable. Mary went to Lincoln School of Art before studying in Paris. She exhibited at the Royal Academy and some of her paintings are in Lincoln's Usher Gallery. Margaret was an author and lecturer, while Ella was a talented sculptor. Ella's work is also on display in the Usher Gallery and, dying a spinster in France, her legacy allowed the Curtois Wing in the gallery to be built.

Artist Thomas Espin, and brothers John and William, were born at Holton cum Beckering, near Wragby. When Thomas was young, he moved with his farmer father to Priory Farm, Bullington. It's said that a stone sculpture of a head in one of the farm's gables inspired Thomas's interest in art.

In 1790, Thomas became a master at Dr Mapletoft's school in Louth, a position he held for thirty-two years until he died suddenly in 1822, aged 56.

During his life, he travelled around the country creating architectural watercolours.

Michael Caine portrayed a member of a Lincolnshire family in the 1964 film *Zulu*.

He played Gonville Bromhead, whose family seat was at Thurlby Hall, near Lincoln. Bromhead was the hero of the Battle of Rourke's Drift in 1879, when he, fellow officer John Chard and 890 soldiers defended the South African post against 4,000 Zulus to prevent the invasion of Natal. Bromhead and Chard were awarded the Victoria Cross.

STUBBS: A SPORTING PAINTER

George Stubbs once resided in the picturesque Wolds village of Horkstow.

In 1758, he leased a farmhouse with niece Mary Spencer to complete a portrait commission of Lady Nelthorpe. He was well known for his portraits among the gentry, and his arrival in the village got people talking.

He made requests for dead horses, spending mornings and evenings dissecting while painting portraits on afternoons. He would make drawings of the carcasses and their skeletons, and used a contraption to suspend the horses and position their limbs, as if in motion. He carried whole carcasses on his shoulders without help to an upstairs room.

Stubbs studied anatomy at York and lectured on the subject. For six years he worked on plates of horses in this way, and in 1766 'The Anatomy of a Horse' brought acclaim. It was the first folio to clearly depict the horse's structure. At his death, his niece inherited the folio and it's now with the Royal Academy.

While in Lincolnshire, Stubbs was paid £20 to paint Sir John Nelthorpe's spaniel at Top Pond, Scawby.

DO YOU DIG LINCOLNSHIRE? STUKELEY DIDN'T!

One of the father figures of British archaeology lived in Stamford from 1718 to 1747.

William Stukeley was a well-known physician and public figure when he arrived to reside at St Peter's Rectory and later a large house on Barn Hill. It was there he wrote a book claiming Christianity originated from the Druids; the first systematic study of stone circles ever written.

As time went on, his beliefs grew obscure and he became stifled by Stamford. One of his notebooks, now in the British Library, reports that he felt the town did not hold 'one person, clergy or lay, that had any taste of learning or ingenuity, so that I was actually as much dead in converse as in a coffin'. He grew bored of Stamford and left for London.

WHAT'S IN A NAME? A FEW MORE PINTS!

John Smith, of Louth, was nicknamed Six Pint Smith for his daily habit of drinking twelve halves of beer before the church clock finished chiming noon.

In May 1818, a fair came to town and Smith wanted to buy goods from a pedlar. He didn't have enough money so challenged the pedlar to a drinking contest. The pedlar was a match for Smith – drinking two pints for Smith's every one. Smith admitted defeat but the pedlar said he would hand over his stock and money if Smith climbed Louth's church steeple.

With ten pints in him, Smith climbed to the top, danced a hornpipe, and paused during his descent to stand on one leg with both arms outstretched; no mean feat considering St James' Church spire – known as the Cathedral of the Wolds – is the tallest medieval example in England, towering 290ft.

Once back on firm ground, he realised the pedlar had disappeared, taking Smith's overcoat. To add to his woe, Smith realised he had left his hat on the steeple. He was about to climb back up when some soldiers took shots at it, so the hat was left there. From then on he was known as Ten Pint Smith instead!

PASSIONATE ABOUT EXPLORATION

Sir Joseph Banks lived in Horncastle in a double-roofed townhouse which still stands on the High Street today. He was a key figure in the construction of the canal in 1802, which gave access to the River Witham.

Sir Joseph voyaged the world with Captain Cook between 1768 and 1771. He was made President of the Royal Society in 1778.

He was born in London on 13 February 1744, the only son of William Banks, of Revesby Abbey. It was while he studied at Eton that he became interested in botany.

Aswarby-born George Bass discovered the Bass Strait sea passage.

When his farmer father died, the family moved to Boston and George trained as a surgeon, joining HMS *Reliance* which sailed to Botany Bay in 1795. Incidentally, Lincolnshire-born explorer Matthew Flinders was among the crew.

George bought a whaling boat to explore the New South Wales coast, discovered there was a sea passage and returned the following year with Flinders. It became known as the Bass Strait.

In February 1803, George sailed for South America but went missing. It's assumed that he died there in 1812.

Matthew Flinders was born in Donington-in-Holland in 1774, and became the first to explore much of Australia's coastline.

He was expected to go into medicine but instead entered the Navy in 1789.

In 1798, Flinders discovered the Kent Group of islands and circumnavigated Tasmania, discovering the site where Hobart, it's capital, is now situated.

In 1801, he reached the south-west coast of Australia and for seventeen months carried out a survey there. When he sailed for home, war had erupted between England and France, and Flinders was imprisoned in Mauritius. There, he started writing *A Voyage to Terra Austral*. He was released in July 1810 and returned to England, and his book was published just days before his death on 19 April 1814.

Rosita Forbes was born in 1893, the daughter of H.J. Torr, of Morton Hall. She began travelling in her teens, married young and was divorced by 1917.

The following year she travelled across the Pacific to the Dutch East Indies and the Far East, and her exploits formed the subject of her first book, *Unconducted Wanderers*, published in 1919.

In 1920 she travelled to North Africa and Arabia, and then to Kufara and Libya, where no European had attempted to reach since 1879.

Rosita made firm friends with Sheikh Sidi Idriss, who supported her to reach Taj, where she lived as a veiled woman, hiding a camera under her cloak. When she returned to England, King George V summoned her to personally hear of her adventures.

She published more books, re-married in 1921 and became a Fellow of the Royal Geographical Society, as well as several foreign societies.

Rosita passed away in 1967, forever a pioneering female explorer.

When Lucy Roberts embarked on a journalistic career, little did she know that she would become a Polar explorer.

Lucy was born in Lincoln in 1968, becoming a reporter and editor. It was during this time that she interviewed Caroline Hamilton, who had an ambition to walk to the North Pole.

Lucy was taken with the idea and beat off competition from 600 hopefuls to join a twenty-strong team of British women to attempt the first ever Polar relay.

She was a member of the fifth and final section, and after ten days' travelling 230km, she reached the North Pole on 27 May 1997.

Ernest Coleman was born in Lincoln in 1943 to a trawlerman, and his family moved to Grantham three years later. A yearning for the sea saw him attend HMS *Collingwood* in Farnham, and at 17 his first voyage was on HMS *Ark Royal*, on which he sailed around the world.

In the Navy, he reached the rank of chief petty officer, served on every type of ship and was awarded a lieutenant's commission. In 1990, he led a two-man expedition to the Arctic in search of Spilsby-born Sir John Franklin's grave.

Sir John's own search for the North West Passage, and his disappearance with 129 men sometime between 1845 and 1848, fascinated Ernest.

In 1990, Ernest trekked to King William Island in the Arctic and found a human skull. In 1992, he returned alone and discovered two man-made mounds, which he is convinced are the graves of Franklin and his colleagues.

LINCOLNSHIRE'S VERY OWN MARTYR

Annie Askew was born in Stallingborough in 1521, the daughter of Sir William Askew. Highly educated and devoted to Bible studies, Annie became a campaigner on the rights and wrongs of the Establishment.

In sixteenth-century England, women had little freedom; Annie's sister was 'sold' to Thomas Kyme, of Kelsey. Before the ceremony, the bride-to-be died and there was only one solution to avoid financial loss – Annie.

Against her will, she married Kyme and bore him two children. She remained outspoken and preached about the injustices of the Established Church in England. Annie eventually left Lincolnshire for London, leaving her family behind.

She joined Protestant Reformers in the city, speaking against transubstantiation, and was in direct contact with ladies of the Court, including Catherine Parr, Henry VIII's last wife. Catherine was actively involved in the Reformation and her beliefs outraged the Catholic clergy. Annie's views led to her arrest for heresy, and in March 1545 she appeared before the Lord Mayor of London and Bishop Bonner, who was said to be responsible for sending 200 Protestants to the stake.

Annie would not be intimidated into confessing to a crime she considered herself innocent of, and even when offered a lifeline through retracting her statements, she refused.

She went on trial but the Church could not procure their witness and she was released. Annie continued to preach and within a year was jailed at Newgate, where she was given one last chance to repent. She refused and was moved to the Tower of London, where she was questioned about her relationship with Catherine Parr.

She knew she faced torture, and indeed was placed on the rack while the questions continued. She was so badly tortured that her captors carried her in a basket from the rack to the stake, in Smithfield, where, aged just 25, she died.

THERE'S NO WORTHIER MAN

Dr Samuel Johnson had close links with Lincolnshire through Bennet Langton, of the old county family from which Langton, near Horncastle, takes its name.

Bennet was born in 1737 and was an avid reader of *The Rambler*, to which Dr Johnson contributed. The pair began corresponding in May 1755, after being introduced in London. Johnson's dictionary was complete and he wrote to his young friend, 'I am at liberty and think of taking the opportunity with this interval to make an excursion, and why not then into Lincolnshire?'

The visit didn't happen, for reasons unknown, until 1764. Johnson caused an amusing spectacle when he rolled down a steep hill, known as the Sheepwalks, behind his friend's house.

They remained close friends, and Bennet is often referred to in Boswell's famous account of Johnson's life. In 1788, Bennet – married with eight children (Johnson was godfather to second daughter Jane), and having inherited the Langton estate – succeeded Johnson as Professor of Ancient Literature at the Royal Academy.

Bennet was at Johnson's bedside before he died in Southampton in 1801, and Johnson said of him, 'The earth does not bear a worthier man than Bennet Langton'.

LUCKY NORMANS GIFTED LAND IN LINCOLNSHIRE BY WILLIAM THE CONQUEROR

Ivo Tallibois received land in Clee, Humberston, Tetney and the Fens. He also built a mansion in Spalding.

The Bishop of Bayeux (William's half-brother) received land in Clee, Itterby and Thrunscoe.

Earl Hugh of Chester (William's nephew) received land in Theddlethorpe, Mablethorpe, Trusthorpe and Sutton-on-Sea.

Count Alan of Brittany (William's son-in-law) received land in Theddlethorpe, Sutton-on-Sea, Addlethorpe and Skegness.

Gilbert of Gent (William's youngest nephew) established a seat at Folkingham with land in Barton-upon-Humber, and re-founded Bardney Abbey. He received land at Mablethorpe, Addlethorpe and Skegness.

Eudo, son of Spirewic, was given the lordship of Tattershall, and received land at Sutton-on-Sea, Addlethorpe and Skegness. His son founded Kirkstead Abbey.

THE IRON LADY

Britain's first female Prime Minister, Margaret Thatcher, was born in Grantham on 13 October 1925.

Her father was a grocer, Methodist preacher and council member. The family lived above their shop in North Parade.

Margaret won a scholarship to Kesteven and Grantham Girls' School, and then went to Oxford. It was there she became the first female undergraduate to be elected chairman of the Oxford University Conservative Association. She became prime minister in May 1979 until 1990, when she was succeeded by John Major.

CLARIBEL'S ROGUE FATHER

Charlotte Alington Pye, better known as Claribel, was a poet who composed popular ballads including 'You and I' and 'Maggie's Secret'.

She was born in Louth in 1830 to well-known solicitor Henry Alington Pye, who built The Cedars in St Mary's Lane.

Her ballads were taken up by London music publisher Boosey & Hawkes and became very popular. Her first recorded poem was written at the age of 9. She published ninety-six songs and was advertised as the most popular composer of the day.

Charlotte married Reverend Charles Cary Barnard in 1854 and they moved to London, where their neighbour was the conductor Michael Costa.

In 1862, on a visit to her hometown, she wrote '20 Spring Songs' and sang some of her works at a concert organised to clear the debt of a new window in St James' Church.

By 1864, she was living in Kirmington with her husband. Four years on, her father fled the country – initially in a rowing boat – for Belgium with his second wife when it was revealed that he had been stealing money left in his care. He later died in disgrace and impoverished.

Charlotte joined him, returning to England in January 1869 for a holiday, but died in Dover from typhoid fever.

SIR ISAAC NEWTON: LINCOLNSHIRE'S SCIENTIFIC REVOLUTIONARY

Scientist and mathematician Sir Isaac Newton was born at Woolsthorpe Manor, Colsterworth, on Christmas Day 1642.

He was head boy at King's School, Grantham, and lodged with an apothecary before going to Cambridge.

He became Master of the Mint and his inventions improved coin manufacturing. He is renowned for discovering gravity and the laws of motion that underpin much of modern physics.

In 1705 he was knighted by Queen Anne, who called him the 'greatest genius in the land'. He died aged 85 and is buried at Westminster Abbey.

MORE LINCOLNSHIRE
INNOVATORS AND PIONEERS

Carpenter and clock repairer's son John Harrison was 7 years old when his family moved to Barrow-upon-Humber, where his father's employer, Sir Roland Winn, had an estate.

In 1715, John constructed an eight-day clock in wood, which is now in the Science Museum.

His marine chronometers – to measure longitude at sea – won a British Parliament award under the 1714 Longitude Act. In 2002, a BBC public poll voted Harrison as 39th in a list of 100 Greatest Britons.

George Boole, the son of a Lincoln tradesman, invented Boolean algebra and wrote two textbooks. At 16, he was employed as a teacher in Lincoln, and then Waddington.

Aged 20, he opened his own school but moved to Cork when he was appointed mathematics chair of the newly founded Queens College. He stayed there for the rest of his life, dying suddenly in December 1864.

Leonard Cheshire served in Bomber Command from 1940 to 1945, becoming group captain and in charge of 617 Squadron. Aged 25, he was the youngest of that rank and completed 100 operations.

He was awarded the Victoria Cross, and was the official British observer when the atom bomb was dropped on Nagasaki in 1945. He was also awarded the Distinguished Service Order with two bars and the Distinguished Flying Cross.

He left the RAF in December 1945 to establish Cheshire Homes for the Disabled. His wife, Sue Ryder, established a foundation for people with disabilities.

In 1991 he was created a life peer and received the title Baron Cheshire of Woodall in the county of Lincoln. He died in August 1992 and a memorial at Lincoln Cathedral was attended by the Duke of Gloucester.

Grimbarian Arthur Flodman landed in Normandy with the Durham Light Infantry. When he appealed for fellow Normandy veterans to meet, twenty-nine people attended the first meeting. The Normandy Veterans Association was officially formed in 1981 and within four years had thirty-five branches across the UK, so Arthur decided to form a national association with his commanding officer, General John Mogg, as president. Arthur died a few weeks later.

Gainsborough's Richard Hammond is credited with inventing the first pedal-and-crank bicycle in England.

He was born in Boston in 1829 and moved to Gainsborough with his family when he was 2 years old. A coach builder by trade, it was in the early 1860s when he became interested in the idea of building a velocipede, first looking at a three-wheeler but soon choosing a two-wheeled design instead. It was road-ready by January 1868, made of iron with wheels measuring 3ft.

The first velocipede machines came over from France in November of that year, so his claim is probably valid. Hammond also invented a dog cart which could carry two people.

'Aaron the Jew' was a famous money-lender and lived on Steep Hill, Lincoln. When he died in 1186, a special branch of the Exchequer was opened to deal with the enormous amounts of money owed to him. A modern-day survey placed him in the top ten wealthiest British citizens ever.

Sir Isaac Pitman, who invented the Pitman shorthand system, taught for some years at a school in Barton-upon-Humber. His system has origins in his first job as a clerk at a textile mill in the early 1800s. He read a dictionary in order to learn the correct pronunciation of words, which led to an interest in phonography.

Aged 18 and after five months of teacher training, Isaac became Master of the British School, teaching 120 boys. He gave frequent lectures to townsfolk on astronomy, became secretary of the Temperance Society and, in 1835, became a Methodist preacher on the Barton Circuit.

He then tried to teach phonography but was displeased with the current systems in place and created his own. He left Barton for Gloucester in 1836 for family reasons, and visited Barton in 1841 during tours to raise the popularity of his system.

A LIFE CUT SHORT

A statue in Boston's market place commemorates entrepreneur Herbert Ingram who, in his 49 years, rose from a butcher's son to respected newspaper founder who brought clean drinking water to Bostonians.

Herbert, born in 1811, was apprenticed to a printer and chemist and moved to London aged 21 to find work as a machine printer.

He made friends with Nathaniel Cooke and they established a printers, newsagent and stationers in Nottingham. Herbert, drawing on his chemist background, used a corner of the shop to stock medical pills.

Somehow the pair met a descendant of Thomas Parr, who was famous for living to the grand old age of 152. Thomas said his long life was due to a vegetable pill; Herbert managed to purchase the recipe and Parr's Life Pills saw himself and Nathaniel make enough to afford a move back to London.

They established a printing business and Herbert, then aged 31, founded the *Illustrated London News* in 1842. The edition reporting on the funeral of the Duke of Wellington in 1852 sold 250,000 copies. For the 1855 Christmas edition, colour prints were used for the first time.

Herbert, by now a father of nine, maintained links with Boston. He was instrumental in restoring St Botolph's in 1853, and formed the Boston Water Works to provide clean drinking water. He also established the *Boston Guardian*.

Flushed with success, he purchased Swineshead Abbey as his family home (it was where King John was allegedly poisoned by monks in 1216) and bought 2,000 acres of farmland.

He was elected MP in 1856, 1857 and 1859. His first campaign was supported by the editor of *Punch* magazine, Mark Lemon, who had lived in Boston as a teenager.

In 1860, Herbert took his eldest son, 15-year-old Herbert, on a trip to America to obtain illustrations for his London newspaper.

As they sailed across Lake Michigan, the ship collided with another. Herbert's body was recovered but his son's was never found.

In tribute, Mrs Ingram funded a new lifeboat in Skegness in 1864, called *The Herbert Ingram*. It was in service until 1874, when it was replaced by a second boat of the same name, again paid for by Mrs Ingram, which was in service until 1888.

BRITAIN'S HEAVIEST MAN

At the age of 39, Daniel Lambert died in Stamford. His passing is remarkable because he weighed almost 53 stone – making him the heaviest man in Britain at the time.

His vital statistics were recorded as 3ft 11in leg circumference; and 9ft 4in around the waist.

Daniel had a physical disorder which caused him to rapidly put on weight from an early age. By the time he was 23, he weighed 32 stone.

He worked as keeper of Bridewell Prison but when that closed, reluctantly decided to exhibit himself in London. He came to Stamford to exhibit himself during the Wittering Heath horse races, lodging at the Waggon and Horses Inn. He died suddenly in 1809, and a window and wall was removed to reach his body. Twenty men were needed to lower the coffin into his grave.

A set of his clothes was displayed for many years at the London Inn, and are now at Stamford Museum. Famously, General Tom Thumb – aka American dwarf Charles Stratton – came to view the clothes, leaving some of his own for comparison.

Daniel entered the *Guinness Book of Records* as 'the most corpulent man of whom authentic record exists'. This was (much) later beaten by Peter Yarnell of East Ham, who weighed 59 stone when he died in London in 1984.

SOME LINCOLNSHIRE CHARACTERS

Recluse Henry Welby, who died in 1636, bought the estate of Goxhill from Lord Wentworth. He led a life full of incident: he married a niece of Lord Burleigh, who sadly passed away, and his half-brother tried to kill him during a disagreement. In about 1592 he became a recluse in London, and only his maid ever saw his face. His diet consisted solely of oatmeal and herb salad, apart from when he treated himself – to egg yolk, crustless bread and beer.

At 4ft tall, Eardley 'Hedley' Broddle was well liked in Mablethorpe. He delivered milk from a cart for a farmer, and cleaned and ground knives for a living. He was a happy sight in the resort, whistling and singing as he went about his work. Born in Louth in 1846, he later returned there and died in the workhouse in 1910.

Talented in music and literature, Joseph Charles Edwards was unfortunately financially useless. He was the rector of Ingoldmells for thirty-two years and, having no relatives, earned his living through begging letters. He died in July 1896 at the age of 82, and an obituary in the *Daily Telegraph* declared him as the 'most notorious begging letter writer in the Church of England'.

James Quanborough – who for more than forty years collected road and market tolls in Bourne – lived frugally. He had no other means of income, and on market days would often be found picking up unwanted vegetables to boil. For fourteen years he did not shave and for the last seven years of his life he did not once leave home. When he died in September 1790, aged 102, £300 was found secreted about his room.

Agricultural labourer James Anderton had nimble fingers. He was known as Cranky Jimmy because he spent ten years constructing a model of Lincoln Cathedral with more than one million corks. After his working day, he would walk the 3 miles to the cathedral to copy it in detail. His task soon became known across the district, and cooks would send him their used corks to help.

He went on to create other models, including a replica of the Scot Monument in Edinburgh. His nickname changed to 'The Patient Man' and his models were displayed at the 1862 Great Exhibition. He died in November 1892.

William Grange was reputedly the oldest town clerk in England, having held the position in Grimsby for fifty-one years. He was born in 1821 and educated at Freeman's Grammar School. In adult life, he was a staunch Methodist and a teetotaller. He passed away on 12 June 1913, at the age of 91, and was buried in Scartho Cemetery.

Psychic Doris Stokes was born in Grantham in 1920, and first visited a medium at the age of 13, where her late father spoke to her. The death of her infant son prompted Doris to join a spiritualist church and, aged 24, she became a medium herself. She achieved popularity around the world, appearing at the Sidney Opera House and other major venues. She wrote for magazines and penned many books before her death aged 68 in 1987.

THE ASTRONAUT WHOSE HOBBY IS... FLYING!

Many youngsters dream of going into space, and one became the first British-born man to walk in space.

Michael Foale, of Louth, was born on 6 January 1957 while his father Colin was working as a pilot attack instructor at RAF Manby. Although his association with the county was brief – the family left when Michael was 15 months old – he has affection for Lincolnshire, and a lane in Louth is named after him.

Michael joined NASA in 1983. He went into orbit for nine days in 1992, following this up with two more space flights. In February 1995, he achieved the distinction of being the first British-born man to walk in space.

In 1997, he joined the Russian Space Station Mir, and survived a collision with a supply ship.

He lives in America, and enjoys flying in his spare time.

SIR JOHN FRANKLIN:
YELLOWBELLY ADVENTURER

Spilsby was the home of Sir John Franklin, who discovered the North West Passage in northern Canada – an expedition which took his life.

His disappearance with two ships and 128 other men remains one of the greatest exploration tragedies.

He was born in April 1786, the youngest son of a family of twelve. He was schooled in Louth, and a childhood visit to nearby Saltfleetby is credited with inspiring his determination to go to sea. His father, a prosperous shopkeeper, did not approve but allowed Franklin, aged 13, to join a merchant trading between Hull and Lisbon, thinking it would put his son off the sea.

It didn't: aged 14, Franklin joined the Royal Navy and saw action in the Battle of Copenhagen under fellow Yellowbelly, Captain Matthew Flinders.

In 1818, Sir Joseph Banks recommended that John take part in a voyage to the Arctic. They spent some time surveying but his ship was damaged by ice, so returned home before winter. Throughout his life, Franklin made various exploratory voyages and was knighted.

In 1845, he set out on his last Arctic journey. The entire crew disappeared. It transpired that Franklin had died on 11 June 1847. The cause was not recorded, and speculation as to what happened continues to this day.

There are statues of Franklin in Waterloo Place, London, and Spilsby, and a monument to him in Westminster Abbey.

MUSICAL PARTNERSHIP
FORGED THROUGH CHANCE

Songwriter Bernie Taupin is the man behind the lyrics of Elton John's 'Candle in the Wind'. Born to Robert and Daphne in 1950, he lived in a rambling farmhouse at Owmby-by-Spital. He credited his storytelling grandfather and famous musician Joe Brown – who was born about 10 miles away – as his childhood inspirations.

Bernie was educated in Market Rasen and became a printer's apprentice with the *Lincolnshire Chronicle*.

It was luck that his musical career took off. He saw an *NME* advert by Liberty Records asking for new writers. Bernie wrote a letter but never sent it; luckily his mother found it, and popped it in the post. His lyrics were read by Reginald Dwight, and it was a 17-year-old Bernie who teamed up with 20-year-old Reg, who would later become known as Elton John, to write music.

Among the songs written during their thirty-year partnership was 'Saturday Night's Alright for Fighting', which was inspired by Bernie's experiences of brawling rockers in Market Rasen and Caistor.

'Goodbye Yellow Brick Road' is also on Bernie's CV; he has written the lyrics for almost 600 songs, the majority performed by Elton.

In a similar turn of events, Rod Temperton, of Cleethorpes, answered an advert in *Melody Maker* in 1974 and joined the band Heatwave. He left after four years and moved to Beverley Hills to write music. Quincy Jones recruited him to write three songs – including 'Rock with You' – for *Off The Wall* by Michael Jackson. In 1982, Rod wrote for Jackson's album *Thriller*, including the title track.

LINCOLNSHIRE'S POET LAUREATE

Alfred Lord Tennyson was born in Somersby in 1809, were his father was rector, and was educated in Louth. He lived there until the age of 28; Lincolnshire is credited with developing his language skills and enhancing his connections with nature.

Tennyson's best-known poems are 'The Charge of the Light Brigade', 'The Lady of Shallot', 'In Memoriam', and 'Maud'.

His father, Reverend George Clayton Tennyson, is buried in a tomb at Somersby. He was the vicar of Grimsby between 1815 and 1831. Alfred's mother was the daughter of Reverend Stephen Fytche, vicar of Louth, and he had an older brother, Charles.

Young Alfred once wrote a rambling and plotless story, which he showed to his grandfather, George, who lived at Bayons Manor in Tealby. George gave him 10s, declaring it would be the first and last time Alfred would make money from writing!

Alfred and Charles's parents were not forthcoming with pocket money, so in later years they published verses to make cash. They took the works to Louth publisher Mr Jackson, who offered £10. When it went to print, he gave them £20.

A copy of this first ever edition of Tennyson's work was found a long time ago on a second-hand book stall in Louth by a Grimsby gentleman; he bought it for fourpence, and after his death it was sold for over £10, such was Tennyson's popularity.

Tennyson succeeded Wordsworth as Poet Laureate in 1850. When he died in 1892, he was buried in Westminster Abbey and mourners at his funeral included Sir Arthur Conan Doyle, Henry Irving, J.M. Barrie and Thomas Hardy.

4

CRIME AND PUNISHMENT

A DEATHBED CONFESSION

Gamekeeper William Dadley was married to his sweetheart for just five days when he was killed by a poacher.

He moved from Norfolk to Well, near Alford, to become head gamekeeper for Robert Christopher MP, who owned Well Hall but lived elsewhere. He was received by Captain Mansell, in residence at the hall, and by Mr Higgins, the agent for the estate, and William quickly gained respect for his hardworking nature.

In January 1839 he married Margaret Brown at St Botolph's Church, in Boston, and they set up home in his cottage near Ulceby Cross.

Five nights later, as the couple held their wedding celebration, the noise of game being disturbed was heard. William (32) went outside, unarmed, with Charles Harrison, of Sloothby. They caught the poachers but a shot was fired and William died.

Poaching was a problem, and farmers and landowners were so concerned about the incident that they offered money for information leading to the arrest of William's murderers, promising a Queen's Pardon to other poachers.

Well-known thief and poacher John Baker, of Partney, was strongly suspected of murdering a gamekeeper at Normanby not long after William died. He was arrested in Candlesby, found guilty of burglary and transported for life. There was not enough evidence to try him for murder, but it was clear the authorities believed him responsible. He was deported to Van Dieman's Land, arriving there in December 1839.

Years later, a deathbed confession provided a new twist to the crime; Stephen Cowley admitted firing the shot that killed William. The passage of time means the facts will never be truly established.

The spot where William died is marked by an inscribed stone memorial.

SLAIN BY A SWORD

In September 1602, Market Rasen was rocked by a vicious murder, caused by a dispute between the 'Lordes and the rest of the inhabitants, concerning the Commons and Libertie in the Towne Fields'.

This led to an altercation in church after evening prayer. Reverend William Storr advised each side to appoint spokespeople to settle the matter. This idea was accepted but the vicar was asked for his own opinion. He was pressed so much that he admitted that he favoured the poorer people involved in the dispute.

The hot-headed son and heir of one of the 'Lordes', Francis Cartwright, retorted, 'The Priest deserveth a good fee, he speaketh so like a lawyer,' and in the Market Place the following day preached that the vicar was a 'scurvy, lowsie, paltry priest'. But for the law, said Cartwright, he would cut the throat of anyone who sided with the vicar, tear out his heart and 'hang his quarters on the May-pole'.

The frightened vicar sought the protection of the magistrates, but was dismissed. He later gave a sermon that contained passages Cartwright thought were aimed directly at him, so his lust for revenge grew stronger.

A week later, Cartwright saw the vicar in town and attacked him with a sword. Mr Storr died from his injuries. Cartwright was arrested but the magistrates accepted bail, and Cartwright disappeared. Friends tried to procure a pardon for him, but he was eventually forced to flee overseas.

The vicar was buried in Market Rasen churchyard.

HAUNTED FOR LIFE: TOM OTTER'S GHOST

In November 1805, John Dunkerley was walking home from the Saxilby Inn, in Dodington, when he heard a man telling a woman to sit down. John hid behind a hedge and witnessed the man repeatedly batter the woman over the head with a hedge stake.

In his hiding place in Dodington Lane, John fainted. When he regained consciousness, he found the stake lying beside him and blood on his hand. Realising he would be framed for murder, he fled.

The woman was discovered and taken to the Sun Inn in Saxilby, where she was laid on the mounting stone. She was identified as the new wife of labourer and poacher Tom Otter; in fact, they had only married on the morning of her death.

Tom (also known as Thomas Temporal) had been working on the enclosure of Swanpool when he made the girl pregnant.

Magistrates ordered them to marry and the ceremony took place on 4 November 1806 at Hykeham Church, with Tom accompanied by two constables.

After the ceremony the couple walked along the road near Drinsey Nook, and while his wife was resting, Tom removed a hedge stake and beat her to death. Tom had failed to mention he was already married.

There was no proof he was the culprit, so he was not charged.

Sometime later, the village constable saw Tom sitting in the window of the Sun Inn. The sun shining through the window revealed dried bloodstains on his sleeve, so Tom was tried and sentenced to hang at Lincoln Castle. His body was to then hang in the gibbet at Drinsey Nook.

After his execution, so many people followed the cart containing his corpse that a bridge collapsed under their weight. John Dunkerley, the terrified witness to the murder, returned home knowing he was safe, and helped haul the body up to the gibbet, when the rope broke and injured his hand.

The murder weapon was displayed for many years at the Sun Inn. Even though it was fastened to the wall with staples, every November it would go missing and reappear at the scene of the tragedy. Eventually, the Bishop of Lincoln ordered that it was burned outside the cathedral walls.

Before he died, the unfortunate John Dunkerley admitted he was responsible for the stake's repeated disappearance. He claimed Otter's ghost would appear and compel him to visit the scene and go through the motions of killing.

The scene of the dreadful incident is now called Tom Otter's Lane, and nearby is Gibbet Wood.

SOME FIRSTS...

Priscilla Biggadike was the first woman to be executed inside a prison, in Lincoln on 28 December 1868, after public execution was abolished. On 30 June that year, her husband Richard came home from work to Stickney, ate a meal and fell violently ill. He died at 6 a.m. the following morning from arsenic poisoning. His widow claimed he had tried to kill himself but she was convicted of murder. Thomas Proctor, the couple's lodger and believed to be Priscilla's lover, was also arrested but there was no evidence against him.

The first known occurrence of a body being gibbeted in Lincolnshire was in 1731. Woodcutter John Keel, from Bardney, stabbed his wife in the throat and chest with a hooked hatchet while in a drunken rage. His corpse was hung at Hoffam Walk, a crossroads between Louth and Muckton.

On 15 March 1817, Elizabeth Whiting was the first person to be executed at the top of Cobb Hall, in Lincoln Castle. The Kirton Workhouse pauper had killed her illegitimate infant daughter.

AND LASTS...

The last public execution at Lincoln Castle was of 20-year-old William Pickett and 24-year-old Henry Carey, who murdered William Stevenson at Sibsey on 8 August 1859.

The last felon to be hanged at Hangman's Ditch – at the junction of Westgate and Burton Road in Lincoln – was labourer William Ward, on 1 April 1814. His crime was stealing cloth and cord worth about £200 from a draper's shop in Mareham-le-Fen.

Ward and his friend Bell were seen by a farmer on a stolen boat in Wildmore Fen, who noticed the vessel was piled high with fabric. Residents arrested the pair, during which Ward tried to shoot them, but the gun failed. It was that action that led him to the scaffold; Bell was saved because he was unarmed.

The last execution at HMP Lincoln was of 34-year-old Wasyl Gnypiuk on 27 January 1961.

The Polish-Ukranian who came to England after the Second World War murdered widow Louisa Surgey (64) in 1960. He had previously lodged with her and returned when destitute, to see if he could stay, but broke in and started drinking.

Louisa's decapitated body was found on an allotment the following day and her head found in a carrier bag about a mile away; Gnypiuk said he had a dream about throttling her, woke up and found her body, and panicked. The jury heard how he had stolen £250 from her, so rejected his claim and found him guilty of murder.

Gnypiuk was a heavy drinker and suffered from mental health problems. He was the first ever condemned man to appeal to the House of Lords, rather than the Home Secretary.

THE SAUCEPAN MURDER AND OTHER UNUSUAL WEAPONS

On 18 July 1809 a man was battered to death in an ill-lit, squalid alley with a three-pint iron kitchen pot.

It became one of the most 'celebrated' of all Grimsby's Edwardian scandals, and the three brothers who committed what came to be known as 'The Saucepan Murder' were fortunate to escape the death penalty.

Victim Alf Day had lived with the only sister of the Ridlington family for four years. There were eight siblings, and her brothers disliked Alf intently.

On the night of his murder, pubs were closing at the Central Market end of the Newmarket Street footbridge.

There strode Alf Day, watched on by Alfred Ridlington, who crouched in a yard off Burgess Street, holding a saucepan. In the street, Percy Ridlington was ready to give his brother the tip-off, and Thomas Ridlington loitered nearby.

At about 10.30 p.m. Alfred struck Alf over the head. The brothers beat him and then left. Alf died within twenty-four hours, and the Ridlingtons were arrested.

They were tried for murder, and the jury took an hour to return a verdict of manslaughter. Percy and Alfred received fifteen years' penal servitude, Thomas three.

Thomas Johnson was executed for murdering an elderly lady, using an iron bedstead as his weapon.

He broke into the home of sisters Elizabeth Evinson and Ann Fairweather, in Croft, near Skegness, in February 1843, tying them to the bedstead while he searched for valuables. He covered their faces with bedsheets while he ransacked the cottage.

Johnson escaped and the sisters remained chained for two days, only rescued when a neighbour heard Ann's cries for help. Elizabeth had died.

Johnson was arrested at Swineshead for passing a counterfeit coin, and silver spoons belonging to the sisters were discovered on him. He was executed on 5 April.

BURNED AT THE STAKE

Eleanor Elsom was burned at the stake for murdering her husband in July 1722.

Because men were considered more valuable in the eyes of the law, if a woman killed her husband, she was not only a murderess, but also guilty of Petit Treason – the betrayal of a superior by a subordinate.

The penalty to a man for committing Petit Treason was hanging, but for a woman it was the stake, the same punishment as for High Treason.

Eleanor's body was tarred and she was taken from her cell in Lincoln to be fastened to a piece of wood and burnt alive. This penalty was abolished in 1790.

THE ACID BATH MURDERER

Serial killer John George Haigh, known as the Acid Bath Murderer, was born in Stamford.

Haigh was executed on 10 August 1949, aged 40, for murdering wealthy widow Olive Durand-Deacon in London by shooting her in the back of the neck and dissolving her body in sulphuric acid.

He admitted committing five similar murders – all to get money or valuables – although it is now thought he could have been responsible for up to nine. Charming and immaculately dressed, Haigh used acid baths to dispose of the evidence. He pleaded insanity, claiming he drank the blood of victims. It took the jury minutes to reject this and find him guilty of murder.

The son of an engineer, Haigh was born at King's Road, Stamford, on 24 July 1909. His parents were strict Plymouth Brethren. They left Stamford around 1916 for Yorkshire, but Haigh frequently returned during the 1940s, often staying at the George Hotel.

Haigh's first prison sentence was for fraud. He was released in December 1935 and became a chauffeur for the McSwan family in London. He also decided to practice as a solicitor, even though he was not qualified, and was jailed for four years.

In June 1941, he was arrested for theft and served twenty-one months in Lincoln Prison. There he worked in a tinsmith's workshop, where sulphuric acid was used. Prisoners who worked on the fields would bring him mice, which he would practice disposing of with the acid.

COVER YOUR EYES!
STREAKER'S OWN LAP OF HONOUR

A streaker who ran onto
the pitch at Blundell
Park told Grimsby
magistrates he did it
because he wanted a house.

The 21-year-old civil engineer,
who was fined £20, ran onto
the pitch during half-time at
the match between Grimsby
Town and Southend in 1975.

Long-distance runner Brian Jones
was about to do a lap of honour at
the interval after running 100 miles
when the defendant ran onto the pitch
for his own version, wearing only a
hat, a scarf round his waist and a pair of red football socks.

He told the court, 'I did it to get publicity.' He was getting married and
his girlfriend was expecting a child, but they could not find anywhere
to live.

THE SERVANT GIRL
WHO CHANGED ATTITUDES

On 13 May 1866, 16-year-old Lucy Sizer was assaulted by five men – and
the resulting court case helped change the Victorian attitude to rape.

Lucy, a servant of good character, was on her way home from
evening service with her younger sister when they were stopped by a
man, Crawford, outside the Dock Offices in Grimsby.

He pulled Lucy towards some railway wagons, clamping a hand
over her mouth.

Crawford knocked Lucy's little sister over and when she refused to
leave, offered her money.

He dragged Lucy into a railway yard shed where he and four other
men – aged between 16 and 25 – each assaulted her. Shockingly, a dock
policeman heard a noise and actually looked inside the shed but went away.

After the brutal rape, two of the youths helped Lucy towards home.
She was ill for some time and suffered serious fits, but she was able to
identify one of her assailants, a man called White. He was arrested and,
scared of taking the blame alone, named his accomplices.

At the trial, the defence alleged Lucy only got the job in Grimsby 'to obtain money for a certain purpose from the fisher lads', but the jury found all five guilty of rape.

Crawford, the ringleader, was given fifteen years' penal servitude and the others were sentenced to six years each.

Early Victorians often treated rape lightly. Cases like Lucy's, in the middle of the era, are credited with it becoming a much more serious offence in law.

ANOTHER WORLD: TRANSPORTATION IN LINCOLNSHIRE

Between 1788 and 1840, 1,200 Lincolnshire criminals were transported to Australia.

John Irvine, who stole a silver cup in Grantham, turned his life around Down Under, and was so respected that a street was named after him.

He was sentenced to seven years' transportation in 1784 and, due to being surgically trained, was sent on the *Lady Penrhyn* convict ship as a surgeon's mate. When he arrived at Sidney Cove, he was employed as a hospital assistant.

In 1790, due to his exemplary conduct, he was emancipated; the first in Sidney Cove. His career saw him posted to Norfolk Island and Parramatta, where in 1792 he was granted 30 acres. He died in September 1795, and a street in Parramatta was named after him.

Transportation was also the making of a Legbourne labourer named Sharpe.

He was convicted in Louth in April 1820 for a crime, and sailed on *The Dick* the same year, arriving in New South Wales in March 1821.

He was well behaved, married well, acquired property and became a gentleman.

Twenty-one years later he returned to Legbourne to find his grown-up son by a former wife, deposited £20,000 in a Louth bank, and went looking for a mansion to buy.

Not all made amends, however. Thomas Tattersdale was transported from Lincolnshire in 1883, and then executed a year later for being involved in murdering Dr Wardell, a former editor of *The Australian*.

TEN WOMEN
TRANSPORTED TO AUSTRALIA

Rebecca Boulton, of Thimbleby, stole from her relations. She gave birth to a daughter on the voyage but died in New South Wales in April 1788, followed by her baby a week later.

Mary Harrison (24) stole bills of exchange from a letter and tried to cash them in Epworth, in 1784.

Mary Groves, from Lincoln, stole money from a house of ill-repute and was transported in 1786. She married fellow transported prisoner William Douglas.

Ann Hall (27), of Heckington, cheated Thomas Obbinson of two gallons of brandy by pretending to be a servant of another house.

Elizabeth Hill (19) was sentenced in 1794 for stealing £29 in gold, one crown piece and two silver shillings from William Green, of Thurlby.

Spinster Ann Smith (31), of Southrey, was transported for burglary against William Holland.

Caroline Coulbeck Lusby (22), of South Elkington, stole a 12-year-old girl's basket.

Eliza Brady (32) kidnapped William Pearson's daughter, in Boston, in 1817.

Priscilla Woodford (16) set a stack alight at Haconby in 1832.

Single mother-of-three Jane Harrison (30) swore in court that John Ullett – the 76-year-old Overseer of the Poor in Bourne – fathered her third child. She was convicted of perjury.

STOP THAT DRUNKEN BICYCLE!

Walter Rilatt appeared in court in Lincolnshire in July 1897, where he was fined a guinea and also given 'rather heavy' costs for drunkenly riding a bicycle.

PC Patchett met the defendant trying to ride the bicycle. Walter said the machine was drunk, not him, and he invited the constable to feel the bike. Unfortunately for Walter, it was he – and not the bicycle – who was punished!

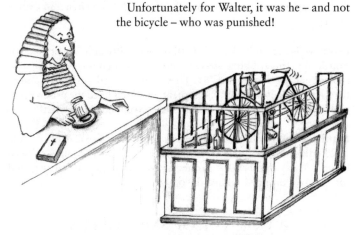

CRIME ON THE HIGHWAYS

Lincolnshire's long and desolate roads were a perfect hunting ground for nefarious highwaymen, particularly in Leasingham, the heaths around Lincoln and Dansby Hill. Noted highwaymen in the county include the following:

William Marshall and Henry Ginn were active criminals from 1737.

Michael Martin, of Fulbeck, was shot dead at Belton Park in 1777 by Dodson and Blades. They were captured in Rutland after robbing a man in Ancaster, and executed in Lincoln.

In 1777, Thomas Ham and William Allen were tried for highway robbery; Ham was executed and Allen freed. Two years before, Ham was sentenced to death for horse-stealing but was instead sent to work on the Thames with a labourers' gang. He escaped and returned to Lincolnshire with criminal intent.

Notorious highwayman Captain Cox was caught in March 1778 stealing a gelding, owned by Squire Charles Chaplin, of Blankney, but was handed a reprieve.

In 1796, Mr Coxon, a deserter from Louth, shot at a Boston butcher on his way home from Stamford Races, stealing a watch and twelve guineas.

Brothers Isaac and Thomas Hallam were brought to justice for murdering and robbing 19-year-old postboy Thomas Gardiner at Holton cum Beckering in 1733. They were arrested in London and as they arrived in Lincoln for punishment, postboys lined the prison route and blew their horns. The brothers were executed and gibbeted.

Many got away with their crimes. On 26 March 1862, robbers stole £122 in gold from John Holmes, of Retford, at Lincoln's railway station. Two suspects were arrested at Peterborough; one escaped and the case was dropped against the other.

A COUNTY OF SMUGGLERS

'Owlers' operated under the cover of darkness along the coast, smuggling goods like wool, which attracted heavy taxes. Officers were employed to prevent smuggling but could be bribed.

One well-known officer went on to much higher things, and is regarded as one of America's fathers. Thomas Paine was posted in 1764 to Alford, a place notorious for smuggling. In 1774, he emigrated to America and became a writer and editor, and is credited with coining the phrase 'the United States of America'.

He was the US Secretary for Foreign Affairs for three years and clerk to the Assembly of Pennsylvania, becoming friends with George Washington, Thomas Jefferson and Benjamin Franklin. He died in 1809.

In 1824, the government cutter *Redbreast* seized a contraband cargo near Wainfleet Haven, capturing three smugglers in possession of 156 tubs of gin, twenty-nine bales of tobacco, two boxes of cigars and a case of playing cards.

Joseph Lowe was landlord of the Scabbed Lamb Inn at Lowes Gap, on the Skegness to Ingoldmells boundary. In 1834, he was fined £1,000 for smuggling. The inn was later washed away by the tide.

In 1826 tallow chandler Thomas Lumley, from Grimsby, was fined £1,500. It's said that New Holland is so named through Lumley, who imported contraband gin in that area. 'Hollands' was a term used to describe Dutch gin.

James Waite, of Ingoldmells, was an infamous Lincolnshire smuggler in the nineteenth century. He was caught many times, but this merely served to give him hero status among the locals. He was so notorious that Skegness coastguards carried his portrait.

A startling discovery was made during renovation work at The Vine Hotel, Skegness, in 1902, when an entombed skeleton was uncovered behind brickwork. On it were scraps of clothing, including brass buttons featuring the royal insignia. It is thought that the skeleton belonged to a revenue man who mysteriously disappeared – probably at the hands of smugglers – 100 years before.

LINCOLNSHIRE MURDERESSES

Arsenic was the poison of choice for 49-year-old Mary Leffey, of Wrangle, when she murdered husband William (59) by peppering his bowl of rice pudding with 135 half-grains (just two grains is fatal). Leffey was executed.

Ethel Lillie Major, from Kirkby-on-Bain, was happily married to 44-year-old Arthur until it emerged that Ethel's younger sister was actually her daughter. The revelation stung Arthur; he turned to drink and, in 1931, Ethel filed for separation. Arthur promised to mend his ways, so Ethel stayed. In May 1934, she found letters from another woman in his pocket. He came home from work, had a meal and then collapsed from what was diagnosed as an epileptic fit. He died two days later. As Ethel prepared for his funeral, a police officer informed her that they'd received an anonymous letter suggesting the death was suspicious. A post-mortem examination revealed Arthur had eaten strychnine-laced corned beef, and he'd ingested a second dose while ill in bed. Ethel was executed on 19 December 1934.

In 1847 Mary Anne Milner, of Barnetby-le-Wold, was accused of murdering her mother-in-law by arsenic poisoning. There was no evidence and she was found not guilty – but was immediately re-arrested, this time for murdering neighbour Hannah Jickels. Hannah's child had died after displaying symptoms of poisoning, and Hannah had the foresight to make a statement before her own death, complaining of feeling unwell after eating pancakes made by Mary. The ingested food contained 30 grains of arsenic. Mary was convicted and was due to be executed at Lincoln Castle, but took her own life in her cell.

ANARCHY IN HIS BLOOD: ARTHUR THISTLEWOOD AND OTHER FELONS

Horsington is the birthplace of Arthur Thistlewood, the leader of the 1820 Cato Street Conspiracy to murder the entire government as they met for dinner. The gang was surprised in their hideout and a government agent was killed.

Thistlewood, the son of a Tupholme grazier, and several other men, including one from Sleaford, were executed. It's said the villain had married an heiress from Lincoln and gambled away her fortune, but there is no record of this.

In July 1893, Elijah Pell, of Great Hale, was arrested for murdering a cat.

He was seen setting his dog upon the animal, which chased it down a drain, where Pell killed it with a hoe.

The cat's owner, William Blackbarrat, said it was worth £1, and demanded he was compensated, but the case was dismissed because the cat's corpse could not be produced.

Captain George Noyce, Market Rasen's Salvation Army leader, was sent to Lincoln Prison for fourteen days for causing a street obstruction. During 1883 and 1884, the town's magistrates objected to the movement holding their meetings in the street.

When Captain Noyce was released, he was greeted by a throng of supporters, who followed him to the market place to witness a rousing speech.

John Greenwood failed to escape the long arm of the law because he was recognised – by his voice.

He broke into John Weatherhog's house in Theddlethorpe in 1831, threatening him with a pistol and then hitting him with it.

Greenwood then beat his victim repeatedly with a poker before stealing money, a silver spoon, a buckle, shot and other items.

Greenwood was stopped by the police and later executed for his crime. He was traced because he was, in fact, the victim's son-in-law who had, until recently, lived at the house. Mr Weatherhog recognised Greenwood's voice, despite attempts to disguise it.

It was May 1859, and a gang of poachers were scouting the banks of the River Witham, near Washingbrough, at about 5 a.m. Henry Enfield had a gun in his pocket, which fell out and blew off the left side of his face, killing him instantly. The incident was witnessed by a guard on the passing Boston to Lincoln train.

THE MACARONI PARSON

A clergyman whose taste for high living saw him dubbed 'The Macaroni Parson' was executed at Tyburn, London, on 27 June 1777.

Dr William Dodd was born in Bourne in May 1729, leaving home aged 16 to attend Cambridge. He was ordained in 1753 and appointed a number of London parishes.

He had an illustrious career; he was Chaplain in Ordinary to King George III in 1763 and made a Doctor of Laws at Cambridge. He also wrote a novel and religious papers, his most famous being 'The Beauties of Shakespeare' in 1752.

His wife once won £1,000 in a lottery – an enormous sum in those days – but Dr Dodd's financial affairs were often in a sorry state. He made the mistake of forging a bond worth £4,200 in the name of the Earl of Chesterfield, his patron. It was accepted but a blot on the signature led the bank to write to the earl to obtain a legible copy.

Dr Dodd confessed and was sent to Newgate, where he wrote 'Thoughts in Prison'. He was found guilty of forgery at the Old Bailey and sentenced to death.

A petition signed by 23,000 people and even letters from Dr Johnson in his defence failed to land him a reprieve.

THE VAGRANT WHO ATE HIS CONFESSION

In January 1904, a homeless man called Fisher was taken to Lincoln Prison. When he was searched, the warder found a notebook in which the word 'Narcissus' had been jotted. The warder assumed Fisher had an interest in flowers and made a comment, upon which the prisoner snatched the notebook, tore out the page and promptly stuffed it into his mouth.

Alarmed, the warder and Fisher struggled a little before the page was retrieved. On it was Fisher's confession of murdering a female hop-picker in Kidderminster.

AN EXAMPLE OF THE LAW CATCHING OUT THE LAW

PC Edward Woods appeared at the Spalding Sessions on 9 July 1892, and was fined £20.

Railway labourer Robert Wright and some young men were returning from a political meeting. As they passed PC Woods, one of them called him 'bright buttons'.

This enraged the officer, who assaulted Wright.

5

LINCOLNSHIRE IN PARTICULAR

SPEAK LIKE A YELLOWBELLY: AN ABBREVIATED A–Z OF LINKISHEER'S DIALECT

Awming	–	Timewasting / being idle
Blatherment	–	Nonsense
Bowak	–	To vomit
Cadge	–	To beg
Daisy-me!	–	To express surprise
Darklins	–	Twilight
Ewt	–	Owed
Flit	–	To move house
Frit	–	Frightened
Gawster	–	Laugh loudly
Hivy-Skivy	–	Confusion
Issen	–	Himself
Jifflin'	–	Fidgety
Kedge-bellied	–	A glutton who has eaten too much
Lig	–	To lie down
Mardy	–	In a bad mood
Mizzlin	–	A cross between mist and drizzle
Nobbut	–	Nothing but
Okkers	–	Heavy boots
Pipe	–	To cry
Quick-sticks	–	Immediately, now
Razzler	–	A very hot day
Reeyak	–	A snowdrift
Scran	–	Food, but of poor quality
Smoot	–	A passage
Tongue-banger	–	A person who nags
Unheppen	–	Clumsy
Vardy	–	Verdict
Werry	–	To give birth
Yauping	–	Noisy / boisterous

ON THE BEAT: WOMEN POLICE OFFICERS

Grantham has the honour of being the first place in Britain to have had female police officers.

In 1914, the Women's Police Service, a voluntary society of women in the market town, was founded to help with cases concerning females.

During the First World War, prostitutes came to Grantham and brothels opened because 14,000 soldiers were based at a training camp in Belton House. This inevitably caused regular public disorder incidents, and the women's voluntary work proved invaluable.

Ex-midwife Edith Smith, a widow with one son, joined the group, having been on patrols in London to gain experience. In Grantham, she soon made inroads into removing the scourge of prostitution. In November 1915, a meeting was held where it was agreed that the women should be supported through public funds and benefit from official status. On 29 November, Mrs Smith was sworn in and became the first professional female police officer in the British Isles.

She used the front room of her home in Rutland Street as a consulting room, and took no days off, no overtime nor a pension. In 1917, for example, she recorded 383 cases, including fifty 'rescue' cases handed over to a social worker; forty 'respectable women helped in court affairs', and forty 'foolish girls warned'. That year she was given a pay rise, bringing her salary to £2 10*s* a week – making her better paid than the oldest constable on the force – but she retired late in 1917 due to ill health. She died in 1924, after taking an overdose.

EDIBLE LINCOLNSHIRE

The county is rich for culinary fans, perhaps because of its agricultural heritage. Here are some well-known Lincolnshire foodstuffs:

Lincolnshire sausage

Cheese, including: Lincolnshire Poacher; Cote Hill Blue; Cote Hill Reserve; Dambuster; Lincoln Blue; and Little Imp

Lincolnshire Haslet

Grantham Gingerbread

Stuffed chine

Lincolnshire Plum Bread

Apples originating from the county include: Allington Pippin; Barnack Beauty; Baron Wolseley; Bolingbroke Beauty; Doctor Clifford; Ellison's Orange; Grimoldby Golden; Ingall's Red; Peasgood's Nonsuch; Schoolmaster; Sleeping Beauty; and South Lincoln Pippin

Lincolnshire Creamed Honey

Samphire

Beef from Lincoln Red cattle

OUR OWN SET OF ANIMALS

There's Lincoln Red cattle, Lincoln Longwool sheep, Lincolnshire Curly-Coat pig, Lincolnshire Buff chicken and Lincolnshire Black horse. Sadly, the Lincolnshire Curly-Coat became extinct in the 1970s. It had a long white curly coat and lop ears, and was generally bred by smallholders. It was one of the oldest breeds of domestic pig in the UK and the last known specimens were kept by John Crowder.

THE MOST FAMOUS LIVING APPLE TREE?

An apple tree stands in the grounds of Woolsthorpe Manor, near Grantham. The seventeenth-century manor, now owned by the National Trust, was where Sir Isaac Newton was born. The tree is supposedly the one which dropped the apple which, in turn, inspired Newton's concept of gravity. He was staying at the manor to escape the plague of 1665 in Cambridge when he carried out his groundbreaking work.

WOODHALL SPA ALMOST DIDN'T EXIST

If businessman John Parkinson had been lacking in entrepreneurial vision, the picturesque town of Woodhall Spa would not exist. Parkinson had ambitions to build a city at New Bolingbroke, plant a forest at Kirkby Moor, and establish a coal mine at what later became known as Woodhall Spa.

But Parkinson became bankrupt, and his city and forest were sold. No coal was found at the mine, which was 1,000ft deep, and it was abandoned in 1824 following a flood.

The shaft filled with water and Thomas Hotchkin, lord of the manor, found the mineral-rich water beneficial for his gout and built a pool room and bathhouse in 1838.

The town was popular for a century until it fell into decline after the First World War.

The 120-bedroom Royal Hydro Hotel and Winter Gardens, built in 1897, was destroyed by two German parachute mines in August 1943.

Golf replaced taking the waters, and its most famous attraction, the Kinema in the Woods, a back-projection cinema, was built in 1922.

SOME PLACE NAME ORIGINS

During our six centuries of rule under the Romans, many immigrants, raiders and settlers made Lincolnshire their home.

This is reflected in place names throughout the county; in fact, it has more than 220 place names ending in 'by' – from the Old Norse meaning a farm or a village centred around a farm – than any other county in England.

For example, the story of Grimsby goes that a fisherman called Grim rescued the son of the King of Denmark from a boat. He called the child Havelock and brought him up. When Havelock grew up and returned to his parents, Grim was rewarded with so much money and goods that he established Grimsby in his name.

Here is a guide to some more place name origins:

Barrowby	–	On a hill
Belvoir	–	Beautiful view
Caistor	–	Derived from the Roman caester, meaning fort or encampment
Conningsby	–	Of the King
Grantham	–	A sandy or gravelly village
Gainsborough	–	Stronghold of a man called Gegan
Lincoln	–	Derived from the Roman 'Lindum colonia'
Norton Disney	–	North settlement of the Insey family
Redbourne	–	Reedy stream
Saltfleetby	–	Settlement by a salt creek
Sapperton	–	Settlement of the soap-makers
Scopwick	–	A sheep farm
Skegness	–	The headland of a man called Skeggi
Skendleby	–	By a beautiful slope
Wigtoft	–	Homestead by a creek
Willoughby	–	By the willows

LINCOLNSHIRE ABROAD

Boston, in the US, is perhaps Lincolnshire's most recognisable overseas twin, but many county place names can be found in New England colonies.

In the reverse, Lincolnshire laid claim to some American names, including New York and Bunkers Hill.

YELLOWBELLY THEORIES: WHERE DID LINCOLNSHIRE'S NATIVE NICKNAME COME FROM?

It is said to derive from the waistcoats worn by the Lincolnshire Regiment.

It came from the fact that the underside of coaches that travelled to Lincoln were painted yellow.

Market women kept a separate purse for gold coins, kept in skirts or aprons, and a good day's trading meant a yellow belly for them.

Farmworkers grafting in a field all day would have brown backs from the sun, but paler stomachs.

Fenworkers grew and used opium to help them ward off malaria endemics. Such medication can turn the skin yellow if used too much.

The term came from the Lincoln Diocese's Elloe Rural Deanery, which took its name from the Saxon administrative division known as Ye Elloe Bellie.

GRIMSBY'S *TITANIC* LINK

Grimsby inhabitant James Paul Moody has a significant place in the history books. He was the sixth officer on the *Titanic* when it sank in 1912, taking his life and those of 1,521 others. The 24 year old was born in Scarborough and living at St James House, Grimsby, at the time of the tragedy. His family included Charles Bartholomew Moody, Grimsby's first coroner.

VISIT A SUBMERGED FOREST

At the end of the last Ice Age, the North Sea was dry land. A forest developed, with alder, lime, hazel, oak and birch trees, but as water levels rose a layer of peat formed around the trees.

These conditions eventually killed the trees, leaving half-buried stumps and trunks preserved in the ground. About 3,000 years ago, the sea covered the stumps but coastal erosion in recent years has resulted in the submerged forest being exposed.

The prehistoric forest can be seen at Cleethorpes, and in 2015 a rare Bronze-Age trackway was discovered in an inter-tidal zone there. It can also be seen at low tide at Anderby Creek and Mablethorpe.

Tools relating to the New Stone and Bronze Age, including flint hand axes, have also been discovered on the coast. A hand axe, found in the 1970s by local conservationist Robert Palmer and officially catalogued by the Lincoln Museum, was made and used at a time which relates to the development of human technology.

TWENTY LINCOLNSHIRE FAMILY NAMES

Anyan	Hutton	Strawson
Brackenbury	Ingle	Thurlby
Cottingham	Lamming	Ullyatt
Dannatt	Mawer	Vinter
Daubney	Odling	Waddingham
Frow	Patchett	Wroot
Grummitt	Reeson	

THE WORLD DIVIDED

Keep a keen eye out when you're in Lincolnshire, because you may find yourself passing from one hemisphere to the other!

In 1884 an international agreement fixed the Greenwich Meridian, which passes through the three Lincolnshire towns of Boston, Louth and Cleethorpes as it travels around the globe, marking the divide between the eastern and western hemisphere.

The Meridian Line also crosses through Kirton Marsh, and the Wash east of the village of Fosdyke.

FRANCIS DASHWOOD'S LINCOLNSHIRE LEGACY

Six miles south of Lincoln, just off the A15 on a public footpath, stands Dunston Pillar. It was erected by Sir Francis Dashwood – the Chancellor of the Exchequer, Post Master General, and he of notorious Hellfire Club fame – in 1751 to guide travellers across the heath and is most probably Britain's only land lighthouse.

In 1745, Dashwood married the widow of Sir Richard Ellis, through which he gained the Ellis estate in Lincolnshire. His home in the county was Nocton Hall, where the pillar was built. The pillar was 92ft high and contained an interior staircase to reach a 15ft-high lantern, which was lit regularly until 1788, when a better road was made.

The lantern was used for the last time in 1808 and fell from the pillar during a storm the following year. In 1810, the Duke of Buckingham placed a bust of George III in the place of the lantern to celebrate the King's Golden Jubilee. The mason, John Willson, fell from the pillar and died. During the Second World War, the height was considered hazardous to aircraft, so King George was toppled and the statue was badly broken.

During his time in Lincolnshire, Sir Francis was a member of the Lincoln Literary Club, which met at the Green Man Inn, 5 miles from Nocton Hall.

IS SKEGNESS IN SCOTLAND? BILLY BUTLIN'S RISE TO FAME

William Heygate Edmund Colborne Butlin – better known as Billy Butlin – thought Skegness was in Scotland.

Born in South Africa and raised in Canada, Billy came to England in 1921 to join his uncle in the amusements business, with just £5 in his pocket. He borrowed his uncle's hoopla and set up shop in Skegness. He had an idea to open an amusement park south of the pier, and by doing so in 1929 he introduced the first dodgems to the country.

He then established a park in nearby Mablethorpe, but it was in 1936, when he opened what is regarded as Britain's first holiday camp just outside Skegness at Ingoldmells, that he became famous.

During the war, Butlin's temporarily became HMS *Arthur*, a naval training ground. After the conflict ended, holidaymakers returned and Billy opened more camps around the country.

Billy was knighted in 1964 and last visited Skegness in 1977, to switch on the illuminations. He died in 1980.

HOW LINCOLNSHIRE SHEEP-SHEARERS COUNT THEIR FLOCK

one – Yan   six – Sethera
two – Tan   seven – Lethera
three – Tethera   eight – Overa
four – Pethera   nine – Covera
five – Pimp   ten – Dic

HUBBARD'S HILLS: A LEGACY OF LOVE

Auguste Alphonse Pahud came to Louth in 1875 to teach French and German at King Edward VI Grammar School. He fell in love with wealthy farmer's daughter Annie Grant. They married twelve years later and lived at The Limes, in Westgate. Auguste retired and the couple spent time travelling. In London in 1899, Annie died suddenly and Auguste became a recluse until his death in 1902. In his £25,000 will, he called on his trustees to fund a £1,000 window in Annie's memory at St James' Church. The Limes became a grammar school for girls and he also ordered that a fund was established to help poor people in Withern, where Annie's parents had farmed. Some money was used to buy Hubbard's Hills from Mr J. Ward, Lord of the Manor at Hallington, for £2,000 and was gifted to the people of Louth in 1907.

THE JOLLY FISHERMAN

In 1936, John Hassall, who created the famed Jolly Fisherman railway poster, made his only recorded visit to Skegness. He was granted with the freedom of the foreshore for the help he gave Skegness in garnering publicity and, in the Jolly Fisherman, a nationally-recognised icon.

His original illustration was presented to Skegness's council in 1965, and a statue was unveiled in 1989. To this day, if you wish to use the image of the Jolly Fisherman, you must pay the council a copyright fee.

SOME ARCHAEOLOGICAL SITES

A Neolithic long barrow is sited between Louth and Spilsby on the A16 at Swaby. There is also a Neolithic field next to the A153 near Cadwell.

There are six Bronze-Age round barrows – the largest being 10ft – at Bully Hills, on the Haugham to Tathwell road. Eleven barrows were excavated south of Willoughby-in-the-Marsh and dated to 1750 BC.

The Iron-Age Honington hill fort is located on the Jurassic Way, which runs along Lincoln Cliff, south of Honington, near Grantham, and also on the A153 Grantham to Sleaford road.

Near the B1176 Bourne road lies the Iron-Age Ingoldsby Round Hills.

The Yarborough Camp is in a wood at Croxton. It was established to guard Kirmington Gap in the Iron Age.

Iron-Age tracks in the county include Barton Street, Bluestone Heath Road and High Street linking Horncastle and Caistor.

Roman roads include the A15 (Ermine Street), A46 (Fosse Way), B6403 near Cranwell, King Street between West Deeping and south of Bourne, and Mareham Lane, north of Bourne. The B1200 between Saltfleetby and Manby is the bank of a Roman road used to transport salt from the coast.

Roman towns include Ancaster, Caistor, Lincoln and Horncastle, and Roman canals include the Fossdyke and Car Dyke.

Wellbeck Hill, near Laceby, and Loveden Hill, near Hough-on-the-Hill, date back to Anglo-Saxon times and the Danes. St Guthlac's Cross on the A1073 south of Cowbit also dates to this time, as do churches in Barton, Ropsley and Stow.

TETNEY: A COMMUNICATIONS HUB

The first radio link between Britain, Australia and India was launched in the small village of Tetney.

Eight masts were erected on Humberston Road in the village and dominated the surrounding countryside, as part of the government's plan to strengthen links between Britain and the rest of the Empire.

It was on 8 April 1927 that the station used pioneering broadcasting methods devised by Marconi's Wireless Telegraph Company. Tetney was chosen because of its flat landscape; it meant the Marconi method of beaming signals on one wavelength only was achievable.

Transmission lines travelled on telegraph poles following the train line from London to Holton-le-Clay, and from there cables were routed through Tetney to the station. It was disassembled in 1940. There was only one similar station in existence, in Cornwall, which transmitted to Canada and South Africa.

The towers were up to 300ft tall and visible from the Wash. Telegrams between Britain and Australia and India all passed through Tetney and Skegness, transmitted by Morse code and relayed to the Post Office Central Telegraph Office in London.

LITERARY LINCOLNSHIRE

Novelist D.H. Lawrence and Lincolnshire, on first inspection, have little in common. However, he was a keen visitor to the area, having first come to Skegness at the age of 16, where his Aunt Nellie (Ellen Staynes) kept a boarding house, called Sandlea. He stayed for six weeks to recover from pneumonia, and wrote home to his sweetheart, Jessie Chambers, that he enjoyed watching the tide from the drawing room.

Later, he returned to Skegness with Jessie and a friend, recording the walks he went on in Trusthorpe and Lincoln. Incidents which took place then were re-told in his novel *Sons and Lovers*.

He also visited Mablethorpe many times, and Lincoln Cathedral is featured heavily in *The Rainbow*.

Four years before he died in Venice, in August 1927, he stayed in Sutton-on-Sea with his wife.

George Eliot stayed at Morton Hall, in the village of Morton, in 1845, and it was here that she began writing her novel, *The Mill on the Floss*. The novel is set in Tofton, the fictional name she gave to Morton.

Charles Dickens described Market Rasen as 'the second sleepiest town in all England'. And the sleepiest town, according to Mr Dickens? Shepton Mallet, in Somerset.

If you were riveted by the adventures of Julian, Dick, Anne, George and Timmy the dog as a youngster, then you may be pleased to learn that Enid Blyton's ancestors were farmers in Lincolnshire for several centuries.

The Blyton family's occupancy of the county ended when Methodist preacher George Blyton gave up farming in Swinderby and became a shoemaker instead.

His great-granddaughter authored the Famous Five, Secret Seven, Mallory Towers and Noddy series of books, to name but a few of Enid's many literary successes.

SOME PARTICULAR FACTS

During the nineteenth and early twentieth centuries, Lincolnshire had about 800 corn mills. A total of 350 of these were tower mills. Sibsey Trader Windmill, built by John Saunderson of Louth in 1887, was one of the last tower mills to be constructed. It is only one of two six-sailed windmills still in existence in Lincolnshire, the other being in Waltham, Grimsby.

The residential houses lining Minster Yard, in the shadow of Lincoln Cathedral, were the first in the city to be given numbers.

Grimoldby Station was the childhood home of actor Donald Pleasance. His father was stationmaster there.

Spalding is home to many glasshouses for flowers and salad crops. Nearby Low Funley accommodates the greatest concentration of glasshouses in the county.

In 1862, more opium was sold in Lincolnshire, Cambridge and Manchester than anywhere else in the country. Crowland was well known for its opium addicts, and Spalding was famed as an opium-eating town.

The level crossing in Cleethorpe Road, Grimsby, was once the busiest in England. It always seemed to be closed as endless trains carrying fish to all parts of the country passed through. It was also the only crossing to be manned by a police officer.

The horse which Wellington rode at the Battle of Waterloo – named Copenhagen – is said to have been bred in Market Rasen.

Did you know that Lincolnshire stored nuclear weapons? Faldingworth Airfield was established in 1940 as a decoy. From 1957 to 1972, it became a secret storage site for nuclear weapons in highly secure underground bunkers. For years it did not appear on maps because of its status.

Every living Shire horse is descended in a direct male line from a stallion bred in Fleet, near Holbeach. The brown Shire, named Wiseman's Honest Tom (sometimes known as Old Honest Tom), was foaled in 1800 by Fleet man William Wiseman. He was sold in 1806 to W. Wood, of Elm, for 400 guineas and Tom sired many successful horses, including England's Glory 705 and Lincolnshire Lad.

A well-known Lutton drunkard was so worried that people would visit the churchyard following his death and say, 'There lies drunken Redhead', that he insisted that his coffin be buried in an upright position. He died in 1770 and there is a memorial to him in the church.

Number 30 South Street, Horncastle, has a death mask over its doorway. It's that of Timothy Brammer, who was also known as Tiger Tim and Rough Tom. Tom was a navvy who worked on the town's canal. He was executed in 1830 for his role in a robbery at a country house. Plaster masks were often made of dead convicts' faces and sold to execution spectators as mementos.

Distant relatives of Lord Byron lived at Cadney, near Brigg, at the end of the thirteenth century.

SOME MORE PARTICULAR FACTS

By the time Henry II was on the throne in 1154, Grimsby was the twelfth largest town in the country, when measured by the level of taxes owed to the Crown.

At All Saints' Church, Lincoln, there is a window through which the altar can be seen. This was to allow lepers, who were not allowed inside the church, to see the altar.

At the grammar school in Spilsby there are etchings above two basement windows in the master's residence. One reads 'cheese' and the other 'dairy', written in white paint. This was to exempt them from the window tax imposed between 1696 and 1851, because they were classed as shops.

The first passenger ferry across the River Humber was the steamer *Magna Carta*, built in 1832 by MS&LR. She was scrapped in 1872 and a larger steamer of the same name replaced her.

Composer Gustav Holst worked in Skegness, playing trombone in the pier orchestra. It's said that he scored the Cotswold Symphony while enjoying the sands of Skegness beach.

The Second Earl of Yarborough, Charles Anderson Worsley, was once said to have bet a thousand to one against the dealing of a hand in bridge or whist containing no ace and no card higher than a nine. This hand has since became known as 'a Yarborough'.

Before barbed wire was invented, farmers would tack hedgehog skins to gateposts to stop cattle from rubbing against them.

In 2003, Grimsby was dubbed 'Winsby', Britain's luckiest National Lottery town. It had seen eleven major wins since the lottery launched in 1994. Experts predicted its inhabitants were twenty-five times more likely to win a fortune than anywhere else in Britain.

Lincolnshire is one of the largest potato producers in the country. So many are produced around Boston that it is known by some as 'Tairtyville'. At Nocton, there was a 4,000-acre estate growing potatoes just for Smith's Crisps and many packets were made at a factory in Lincoln when it opened in 1938.

Prince Charles was once a resident of Lincolnshire. In 1971, he spent five months studying at RAF College Cranwell as a flight lieutenant, and had a reputation for being a joker. Once, he announced over the tannoy system that a fault had been found in the design of the shoes worn by officers, and could they please hand them in to the Porters' Lodge. It took three days for people to realise it was a prank.

If you come across a violin made by Richard Hudson or his son George at a low price, snap it up. Mr Hudson Senior opened a music shop in Skegness in 1878, and with his son, a violin-maker, soon found fame in their well-crafted instruments. They are now collectors' items.

Violet van der Elst, the inventor of face creams including the Shavex lotion, indulged in extravagant tastes when she bought Harlaxton Manor, near Grantham, in 1937. She promptly renamed it Grantham Castle, filling it with antique furniture, including some from Buckingham Palace, and carpets from the Winter Palace in St Petersburg. She sold the majestic property in 1948.

In 1898, you could go underground for a toilet break in Skegness. Subterranean lavatories opened in Lumley Road thanks to a £500 loan from the government. They remained in use for a century until 2001, when they were replaced.

Grimsby's inhabitants lined the streets and bowed their heads in respect on 23 September 1901, when a funeral procession for the victims of the HMS *Cobra* disaster made its way through the town.

The torpedo boat destroyer was on her way to Portsmouth from builders in Newcastle to be commissioned when she was lost off Cromer, having struck the Gudgeon Rocks.

Twelve members of the crew, including the chief engineer, were saved; forty-four Navy officers and men were drowned, and twenty-three contract staff. Six of the perished men were brought to Grimsby and their funeral held in the town, itself sadly no stranger to maritime tragedies.

A TRAGIC LOVERS' PACT

It was October 1922, and holidaymakers had long vanished from the beaches of the Lincolnshire coast. So there was no one to see Thomas Hayter and Annie Ostler take their last steps as they walked, hand-in-hand, onto an empty stretch of beach between Cleethorpes and Skegness.

No one saw them as they faced each other to make their tender farewells, nor saw Thomas remove the sawn-off shotgun from beneath his coat, shooting Annie dead before turning the gun on himself. It was a lovers' pact, and their footprints in the sand were certain proof of their final moments.

Thomas, a mechanic in Grimsby, lived in North Thoresby with his wife and infant child. They lived with the village cobbler, Albert Ostler and his wife, who were Annie's parents.

Mrs Hayter fell ill and despite devoted care, she was taken, with her child, to Grimsby's hospital, where they died. Widowed Thomas, 43, left his lodgings to a new home nearby, and it was from there on this day that he said he was going to Grimsby to catch the London train. Later, he and Annie, 21, were found dead at Sutton-on-Sea, a wedding ring on Annie's finger.

The inquest was straightforward, but there was a twist. Thomas was recognised in a newspaper report in the London Press – by a woman claiming to be his wife.

She said they had married in 1917 and had a child, but Thomas had deserted her. Had he been to London and refused a divorce, and married Annie bigamously? The truth may never be known.

6

CURIOUS LINCOLNSHIRE

THE MYSTERIOUS SCIENTIST

A hunt was launched in February 1894 for a mysterious man who conducted experiments with a strange concoction in Lincoln.

The incident was deemed so extraordinary that the *Lincolnshire Echo* published a police appeal after a Mr Duncombe visited an engineering foundry.

He appeared respectable, aged about 60, and said he was from Bridlington. He showed the foundry a fluid he claimed would work a gas or oil engine – without gas or oil.

'The firm is not one to turn away anything good in the invention or discovery line, and it was decided to give a trial,' reported the newspaper. Mr Duncombe refused to disclose what the mixture contained, but a trial went ahead and the results were good.

The second day did not go as well; although denied by the firm, an eyewitness said there was an explosion and Mr Duncombe stood by 'trembling like an apsen leaf and deathly white'.

The experiments were discontinued and Mr Duncombe admitted the contents were dangerous. He left for Hull, after exchanging a £5 cheque for gold at the Driffield Bank. It transpired he didn't have an account at the bank, and he hadn't paid his hotel bill. The police were informed, but nothing more of the mysterious Mr Duncombe was reported.

SERVANT GIRL SIMPLY DISAPPEARED

The disappearance of servant Fanny Clarke, who was sent on an errand by her mistress and never seen again, caused anxiety in 1870s' Lincoln.

The 17-year-old shepherd's daughter was in service with ironmonger Mr Moody and was sent to Mr Blackburn's bakehouse, near St Martin's Church, to borrow bread tins.

The *Lincolnshire Chronicle* said Mr Blackburn Junior received the girl, who 'stated her business in a jocular manner', adding: 'If you was a man you would take them (the tins).'

The young man said Fanny should, but she said she had another errand. She left the bakehouse, and was never seen again.

Fanny had a soldier lover, but the newspaper stated: 'He has seen nothing of her since April. No reason whatever is assigned to her disappearance. She was on tolerably good terms with her master and mistress, and also with her parents.'

OFF WITH HIS HEAD!

Police officers in 1963 were left scratching their heads over what to do with an unusual item of lost property.

A workman walking through Grimsby's Railway Street glanced at some wasteland and saw… a skull. Shocked, he gingerly picked it up and took it to a police officer in nearby Kent Street.

But officers made no attempt to find the man who had lost his head – a doctor estimated the skull to be about 200 years old.

It was thought the relic had been buried but recently disinterred. It was later destroyed.

WALLY THE WAYWARD WALLABY

When Wally the wallaby went walkabout, he prompted stares of disbelief!

Railway worker Peter George thought he'd had too much Christmas spirit when he spotted the wayward wallaby hopping across a Lincolnshire field in December 1987.

'A farmer called me across and said, "Look in that field and tell me what you see",' said Pete. 'I said I thought it was a kangaroo and he replied, "Thank God, I thought I was seeing things!"'

Pete chased Wally into a nearby wood but even a police dog couldn't flush him out.

The next morning, Pete arrived at work to find Wally cowering in a corner of his station. He was promptly rescued by his owners, Alan Brett and Jean Chappell. Jean said, 'We kept him in a shed but he got out.'

TWO CURIOUS INCIDENTS IN THE 1930s

There was an uneasy feeling among those frequenting the Clee Crescent area of Grimsby at night. They were being attacked by a mysterious entity swooping down silently on their heads.

Five residents experienced the attacks in May 1935 – always between 11.15 p.m. and 11.30 p.m. – with one even hearing ghoulish chuckling.

Each was left with marks and scratches on their heads, evidently made by talons, and it was suggested the culprit was a giant owl.

Ruth Mumby, of Humberston, said, 'My hat was knocked off, my head scratched and the hair nearly pulled out of my head. I swung round to see who, or what, my assailant was, but could see nothing.' She was too frightened to investigate.

Immediately after being attacked, two male victims saw a large bird flying away.

An interested party who frequented that area said he often heard shrieks from owls, which sounded like a child crying.

Weird happenings in Holton-le-Clay so spooked women and girls that they were nervous to venture out alone.

The manifestations in 1938 took the form of flying bottles and bricks, with stones and pebbles landing on roofs and through windows.

Villagers formed parties to discover the cause of the trouble, armed with torches and weapons.

Mr Lamb received a severe wound from a flying stone, and Arthur Thompson was confined to bed as a result of his experience. Miss Atkinson fainted when a shower of stones descended on her bungalow.

One villager went out with a shotgun and although he fired, he contacted only thin air. Mr Brocklesby claimed to have seen a figure in some bushes while on watch with his fierce Labrador. A couple of bottles floated through the air soon afterwards.

The trouble occurred between dusk and 10 p.m. on fine nights only, and lasted weeks. The 'ghost' was not caught.

WHAT DID CAPTAIN SCHAFFNER SEE?

It was September 1970 and Captain William Schaffner, an American RAF pilot, climbed into his Lightning jet fighter plane at RAF Binbrook.

The experienced 28 year old was in such a rush to get in the air that he stopped ground crew from fully refuelling the craft.

Radar had traced an object 37,000ft over the North Sea, travelling at 900mph. The object vanished, only to reappear off the coast of Denmark moments later.

Jets were scrambled and when further assistance was requested from RAF Binbrook, Captain Schaffner responded. He took off at 10.06 p.m. and headed up the coast to a rendezvous point at Whitby.

The pilot reported that he'd made visual contact with a conical-shaped craft giving off a bluish bright light, which hurt his eyes. There was another object close by, which looked like a football made of glass.

The craft turned towards him and Captain Schaffner took evasive action.

At this point he lost contact with radio operators, but they could see two radar blips, moving at 500mph. The blips merged into one and came to a standstill. After a moment, the merged object accelerated to 600mph, then split back into two. One vanished off the screen at a staggering 20,400mph.

Contact was re-established with Captain Schaffner, who reported seeing lights in the sky and feeling dizzy. His plane had experienced a mechanical failure and he was ordered to carry out a controlled ditching. Another aircraft was sent to assist and located Captain Schaffner's craft just off Flamborough Head. The cockpit canopy was open but as the rescue plane made another pass, this time the canopy was closed.

The Lightning sank and was located by divers three weeks later, who reported that the pilot was in the cockpit, but when it was brought to the surface, the plane was empty. Captain Schaffner had disappeared.

The incident occurred at a time of many UFO sightings, including an 180ft-long object surrounded by glass balls over Donna Nook, and triangular objects diving into the sea.

Official documents say Captain Schaffner tried to intercept another plane but was flying too low and crashed.

THE CASE OF THE VANISHING HUSBAND

On what should have been the happiest day of her life, a Lincolnshire bride was left heartbroken following the disappearance of her new husband.

The couple married before family and friends, and the party returned to the bridegroom's home for dinner.

As they toasted the happy couple, the bridegroom's servant drew him to one side and explained there was a stranger at the door, wishing to speak to the master.

The newlywed duly attended to the stranger... and was never seen again. A search party found no trace of him. The incident happened in about 1750.

HAVE YOU HEARD ABOUT
THE GARDEN GNOMES?

In June 2003, fourteen homeowners in Brattleby awoke to find that garden gnomes of all shapes, sizes and colours had arrived.

A year later, thirteen residents received anonymous letters asking them to give good homes to gnomes. They looked outside to see more gnomes, and some sporting types duly displayed them.

In 2005, four gnomes were discovered sitting in a pansy bed under the village sign, and that Christmas, twenty queued at a bus-stop.

Their arrival, by now, had attracted worldwide media attention – and not once had the culprit ever been caught. This went on for ten years until 2013, when all was revealed.

Mourners at the funeral of popular Brattleby resident Peter Leighton found themselves laughing at the service when his son, David, revealed his father was the gnome-loving prankster.

The 61-year-old civil servant, who battled cancer for eight years before his death, even left a gnome at his own home to avoid detection.

His wife Erica and son David were in on it, and although Erica left them to it, David and a friend acted as Peter's accomplices.

Peter loved knowing the gnomes made people laugh. Many were donated to a dedicated collector in a neighbouring village.

FROM A PLAGUE OF GNOMES TO A SCOURGE OF SHOES

Between December 2004 and March 2005, Jason and Claire Foster were the victims of a very strange kind of fly-tipping.

The couple lived in a remote farmhouse near Market Rasen and were confused and unsettled when, almost every Sunday, someone began dumping shoes at the property.

There were matching pairs and single shoes of all types and colours, some cheap and some designer... even a pair of rollerblades.

Determined to find out what was going on, they rigged up a camera and video footage captured the culprits – an elderly couple in a green-coloured car.

INVASION OF THE PHANTOM SCARESHIPS

The public were excited – and terrified – by an invasion of phantom airships.

Sightings of these mechanical monsters, also known as scareships, were widely reported around the UK for some years from 1909, including sightings over the Wash, Lincoln and Immingham Docks.

It was suspected that they were on spying missions and caused concern among the general population.

In May 1909, a gentleman was visiting Burghley House when he heard the buzz of an engine above him. He looked up to observe an oblong cigar-shaped object with lights.

In February 1913, the steamer *City of Leeds* was leaving the mouth of the River Humber when the crew saw something in the sky over East Yorkshire, shaped like 'a shark', with wings and a tail.

The airship had no lights but was clearly illuminated by a full moon. The crew observed it for five minutes, and the airship then headed towards Grimsby.

ONE GIANT AND A GIANTESS

Ann Hardy, of Rippingale, was just a teenager when she died in July 1815, holding the title of the tallest woman in Britain: at over 7ft tall, she was known as the Lincolnshire Giantess.

By the age of 13, she was already 6ft 1in and was exhibited at country fairs as a phenomenon. At the time of her death, aged 16, she was 7ft 2in – the tallest woman in Britain. Her coffin measured 2ft 7in across the shoulders.

The man dubbed the Lincolnshire Giant was Joseph Neal Sewell, who was 7ft 4in tall.

He was born illegitimately in Scamblesby in February 1805, and made his way in the world by exhibiting himself as a curiosity; aged 14, he weighed 20 stone and was put on show as a 'fat boy'.

When he was about 21, he developed a fever while visiting Swansea and was permanently blinded. He recovered in a poorhouse, and set off again on his travels around the country.

Joseph died at the age of 24 on 4 July 1829, weighing 37 stone. His shoes were 14.5in long and 6.5in wide.

In life, Joseph was horrified by the idea of being medically examined after his death, and his friends turned down many cash offers to respect his wishes. He was buried in Taunton and steps were taken to protect him from bodysnatchers.

Chief mourner at his funeral was a dwarf from Somersetshire, who was 37in tall.

ANIMAL CRACKERS

In May 1880 at Epworth, a chicken hatched with two bodies and one head.

On 10 June 1976, a male foal was born in Hibaldstow with a white coat and black stripes. He was named Zebradia.

In December 2006, an albino seal pup was washed up at Sutton-on-Sea. He was named White Beam by staff at the sanctuary which rescued him.

On 31 October 1862, excavations were being carried out underneath a tavern in Spittlegate, Stamford, when workmen found a live toad entombed in bedrock 7ft underground.

A cat gave birth to a kitten with two heads, two joined bodies, eight legs and two tails on 13 April 1802. The cat, which belonged to Mrs Pollard, of Stamford, went on to have another litter, producing a kitten with the same affliction.

DID AN ANGEL VISIT STAMFORD IN 1658?

Shoemaker Samuel Wallis, who had suffered from consumption for thirteen years, heard a knock at his door.

His nurse was out, so with great difficulty he answered the door to a white-haired and bearded gentleman holding a white stick, who was bone-dry despite there being heavy rainfall.

Samuel invited the old man inside for refreshments and after a while the stranger asked the shoemaker what was ailing him.

He suggested that Samuel take a remedy of two leaves of red sage and one leaf of bloodworte soaked in beer.

Samuel thanked the stranger for the advice and offered food, but the old man replied, 'The Lord Jesus is sufficient for me', and left, never to be seen there again.

Samuel tried the remedy and recovered, prompting excitement among Stamford residents that he may have been visited by an angel.

THE DANCER AND THE GEESE

A dancer caused a stir in Lincoln in July 1850, in a rather unusual fashion.

The dancer, Mr Campbell, was a member of a theatrical group and, accompanied by a band and a number of smaller boats, was conveyed in a wash tub pulled by geese from the old gas house in Newland to the old swing bridge at Brayford Head.

Alarmed by the noise of the band and the crowds which assembled, the geese decided they wanted to be set free. The struggle almost capsized the wash tub, with Mr Campbell inside.

The *Lincoln Scrap-Book* noted: 'The two geese were unharnessed before a serious mishap occurred. The performance at the theatre that night was very well attended.'

LINCOLNSHIRE AND DICK TURPIN

Lincolnshire played a part creating Dick Turpin's legacy; the crimes he committed while living at Long Sutton, near Spalding, led to his eventual execution in York.

The legendary felon moved to the area to escape excise men in 1737, staying at the Bull Hotel and later renting a cottage. He assumed the identity of horse dealer John Palmer (his mother's maiden name), trading in stolen stock.

His first recorded crime in the county was the theft of a gelding from Charles Townsend, the curate of Pinchbeck, in 1738. He left the horse with his father in Essex, which caused a stir among the locals, for the acquisition of a new horse was a novelty. His father was charged with stealing the horse, but informed on his son.

Meanwhile, a magistrate issued a warrant for his arrest on a charge of sheep stealing but Turpin knocked out the arresting officer and escaped to Yorkshire. His famous horse, Black Bess, died during the journey.

En route, he stole three horses from Thomas Creasey, of Heckington. On 2 October 1738, he was arrested for disorderly behaviour in Brough and was sent to Beverley's House of Correction, riding there on a stolen horse. He was eventually sentenced to death for his crimes and hanged at York on 7 April 1739.

THE BRIDGE WITH NO WATER

An unusual bridge, too narrow to carry anything larger than a horse, can be found in the centre of Crowland. The construction, built in the thirteenth or fourteenth century, allows three roads to meet over three arches – and nothing flows through them. It is understood that it was once where two streams merged and did operate as a bridge, but now no water flows because of drainage modifications.

ECCENTRIC HENRY'S WILD WALKS

Crowland farmer Henry Girdlestone was an eccentric and popular chap.

In February 1844, aged 56, he made a wager – that he could walk 1,000 miles in 1,000 hours. After a month of walking, Henry became delirious and his concerned friends told him to quit.

Stubborn Henry refused and four days later, returned to his starting point, the Abbey Hotel, having walked 1,025 miles in 1,176 hours. He ate a hearty meal and slept soundly for three whole days.

The experience did not put him off further challenges. On his 60th birthday, he walked a 60-mile round trip in moonlight. Many walked beside him for company, and on his return, the Crowland Band played 'The Good Old English Gentleman'.

SPIRIT IN THE SKY

On 16 July 1912 pioneering British aviator Gustav Hamel landed his plane at Love Lane Corner, Grimsby, having achieved the first flight across the Humber.

He flew from Hull at 2,000ft, to avoid sea mist, in sixteen minutes. Gustav spent a triumphant two days in Grimsby thanks to the *Daily Mail*-sponsored stunt.

Born in 1889, Hamel was prominent in early aviation history and was taught to fly in France at the age of 21.

His best-known exploit was a flight between Hendon and Windsor in eighteen minutes, delivering the first official airmail to the Postmaster General. Among the delivery was a postcard he wrote en-route.

On 2 January 1914, he flew with Miss Trehawke Davis, who became the first woman in the world to experience looping the loop.

Hamel went missing over the English Channel on 23 May 1914, while returning from Paris in a Morane-Saulnier monoplane he had just collected.

In July, the crew of a fishing vessel found a body in the Channel. They did not retrieve it but the description matched that of Hamel. No trace of the aeroplane was found.

THE LIFE-SAVING DOG AND OTHER TALES

Henry Stone, of Skellingthorpe, owed his life to his dog. One afternoon in 1690, they were out walking when a thunderstorm broke. Mr Stone sheltered under a tree, but his dog dragged him out into the open air. Bemused, Mr Stone returned to the spot but the dog once again pulled him away. As this happened a third time, a bolt of lightning destroyed the tree, killing a pheasant sitting in one of the branches.

Mr Stone was so indebted to his dog that he commissioned its portrait, which can be seen today at Doddington Hall. On his deathbed in 1693, Mr Stone instructed that he was to be buried close to the churchyard wall, so when his dog died, they could be near each other.

In June 1814, Stamford youths King and Richards climbed the steeple of All Saints' Church as the bell was ringing. It took them just twelve minutes. Richards hung his waistcoat on the weathercock and the pair safely descended. The lad's waistcoat remained in place for some time afterwards.

Buffalo Bill brought his Wild West Show to Lincolnshire in September 1903 and again in June 1904, with Annie Oakley and The Real Deadwood Stage in tow. They travelled around the county in three trains, arriving in Spalding on 23 September and setting up in a field in Pinchbeck Road. Two shows were staged, with 14,000 people attending each one. And that day was even more notable, for two Sioux Indian babies were born! The following day, the performers travelled to Boston, setting up in Ryan's Field. In Lincoln, their camp was at Carholme Racecourse, and they were disappointed when *only* 8,000 people attended. Admission prices were 1*s*, 2*s*, 3*s* and 4*s*, with box seats at 5*s*, and 7*s* 6*d*. Off they went to other areas of the country before returning in 1904, this time to Highfield Farm in Gainsborough on 29 June, and then the old artillery field in Clee Road, Grimsby, on 30 June.

In 1790, a matter of romance was sorted out with a bout of fisticuffs. A boxing match was held between two women at Waddington. Susanna Locker and Mary Farmery were fighting for the affections of the same young man; Mary won the fight.

January 1860 saw reports of two mysterious occurrences at sea. The schooner *Rover* was brought into dock at Grimsby, having been discovered floating, with the fire burning and a lamp on in the cabin – and not a single soul on board. The brig *Favourite* was found drifting and also brought into Grimsby. The only person aboard was a small boy, almost dead from starvation.

Wife and mother Emma Smith was buried alive for 101 days 10ft below ground in September 1968, for charity.

She emerged from her underground coffin in Skegness wearing a fur coat and sunglasses, looking every inch like a Hollywood star... and all she wanted was a hot bath.

In March 1736, a case of wife-selling was reported in the *Stamford Mercury*.

A man sold his wife to another for one guinea, delivering her with a halter around her neck. Sometime later, the man demanded his wife back, but the buyer refused.

The man took court action against the buyer for detaining his wife, but the jury gave a verdict in favour of the buyer.

SUPERSTITIONS AT SEA

Fishermen and trawlermen are a superstitious lot. Taboo words while at sea in times gone by include:
Rats – referred to instead as Long Tails
Rabbits – known as Bob Tails
Pigs – known as Curly Tails

It was unlucky to whistle at sea because it would call up a dangerous wind.

7

CUSTOMS, FOLKLORE AND MORE

SOME LINCOLNSHIRE CUSTOMS

You'd be forgiven for doing a double-take if you were in the Isle of Axholme on the day of the Haxey Hood.

Every Twelfth Night, the game is played in a muddy field, with copious amounts of beer consumed to boot.

The Hood dates back to the thirteenth century, when high winds whipped the hood from Lady Mowbray's head. It was captured by a group of farmworkers and the noblewoman was so grateful she supposedly gifted land and money. This evolved into the Haxey Hood, and it has been played ever since.

It begins by the Fool and the Lord (who is also a Chief Boggard or Boggin) touring pubs inviting people to take part. On the day itself, the Fool dresses in a flowered hat, clothes adorned with red patches, and warpaint. The Fool and the Lord are accompanied by eleven Boggards or Boggins, and they call into pubs before making their way to the churchyard.

There, the Fool stands on a stone and makes a speech while damp straw is lit underneath him to smoke him out – a safer method than the original, where the Fool was strapped to the branch of a tree, swung over the fire and dropped in!

The party then moves to the field and the hood – a 2ft-long leather-wrapped sausage – is thrown into the crowd. The race is on for teams to get the hood into their assigned pub. The winning landlord keeps the hood on display until the following year.

In the past, the game's rough and tumble has destroyed stone walls and hedges, but part of the Boggards' job is to ensure no one is hurt in the scrum, which normally lasts a minimum of two hours.

A bad-tempered schoolmaster thrashed a boy, stringing him to a washing line by his thumbs. The villagers of Holton-le-Clay were outraged so they 'ran-tanned' the teacher. They gathered pots, pans, kettles and a huge piece of sheet iron and, armed with sticks and hammers, proceeded to the schoolmaster's home, led by a Straw Man – literally, a man covered in straw. They ran-tanned the schoolmaster, causing a persistent din outside his house for three nights, before burning the straw outside the pub. The last recorded ran-tanning – usually reserved for wife beaters – occurred in Washingborough in 1910, however, this is believed to have been a re-enactment rather than an actual punishment.

By Victorian times, kissing the Old Man at Stamford School was an engrained custom, although its origins are unknown. The new boys' initiation ceremony took place during the Saturday break. Two prefects would hold each boy up in turn to kiss the Old Man, a medieval carved head on the keystone of a door into the school. In later years, it was only used when a boy had done something to dishonour the school. By 1961, the tradition was abolished.

Stamford, alongside Tutbury in Staffordshire, indulged in the 'sport' of bull-running, similar to Spain where bulls freely roam the streets.

Folklore says the trend originated in 1209, when William de Warrenne, Lord of Stamford, witnessed two bulls fighting over a cow. A butcher and his dog intervened, meaning one of the bulls escaped into the town, where it tossed inhabitants. William mounted his horse and chased it, enjoying it so much that on 13 November each year, he ordered the town's butchers to provide a mad bull in return for grazing rights. However, its true origin is the subject of much debate.

By the 1820s, interest was waning and people began to oppose it.

ARE YOU A CLOCKPELTER? MORE LOCAL LEGENDS

When sheep in a field make a great din or noise without any apparent cause, it will rain.

People from Great Gonerby are referred to as Clockpelters. Tradition saw young men stand at the pond and throw stones at the church clock; anyone to hit it was judged as having reached manhood. The abused clock was also tormented by schoolchildren, who would pelt it with stones or snowballs to make the hands stop.

Grimsby's one-time parish sexton Ned Pearson earned the nickname Old Bluebeard – because he could predict a death. He would hang about a house for some time when he expected the Grim Reaper to appear.

Tom O'Lincoln was a foundling in Lincoln. Folklore says he was the illegitimate son of King Arthur and called Tom after the cathedral bell of the same name. He married Anglitora, the daughter of Prester John, and had two sons, known as Blacke Knight and Fayre Knight. Tom became known as the Red Rose Knight and when he died, the cathedral bell was rung in his honour.

It was custom in Lincolnshire to bind the feet of a corpse to stop the dead returning or prevent it from being possessed by another spirit. Folklorists Gutch and Peacock recorded the story of Old Will Richardson, of Croft. After he died, his wife forgot to tie his feet. A few weeks later, a visitor called at the house to find his widow in a state, convinced her husband had returned. The visitor entered the house to find a toad sitting under Old Will's chair.

On Michaelmas Eve, the Devil goes round and spits on blackberries, making them unfit to eat.

If the day is fine but cattle eat enthusiastically, the weather will turn later in the day.

EGG ROLLING AND MINCH PIES: CUSTOMS AND TRADITIONS BY AREA

Barton-upon-Humber: Egg-rolling day was held at Eastertide. Children would take coloured hard-boiled eggs to the top of a hill and roll them down, before eating them.

Bourne: A curious custom has been practiced in Bourne every Easter since 1770, when Richard Clay bequeathed land (the rent of which was to be laid out in bread for the inhabitants) and the meadow let from year to year in a very singular way. An auctioneer sets off a number of boys on a run. People who wish to rent the field can only bid during the time it takes the boys to run the set distance.

Donington-on-Bain: Old women would gather in the nave of the church during weddings and pelt the bridal party with hassocks, the cushions used for kneeling in prayer. Once the party reached the chancel, the women would throw hassocks at each other. This custom was tolerated until 1780, when Mr Veners became rector. During the first wedding he officiated, the women assembled as usual but a hassock accidentally hit the rector. The custom promptly ended!

Gedney: In 1842, a unique custom was observed. A widow with four children married her new partner wearing nothing but a sheet. This indicated that her husband was not liable for any pre-existing debts of his new wife.

Grimsby: On Christmas Day in 1911, swimmers plunged into Grimsby Dock, in what would become an annual tradition. This first ever dip took place in the morning; afterwards participants dried off and went their separate ways for a hearty dinner. Sometimes they would have to break surface ice before being able to take a chilly dip. Past local dippers include Channel swimmer Hayden Taylor and Pete Winchester who, in 2013, completed his seventieth swim of the River Humber and is known as the Humber King. Swimmers also see in the new year with four minutes, two either side of midnight, in the water at the docks and at Cleethorpes.

Gunthorpe: Christmas carols were sung between 5 a.m. and 7 a.m. on Christmas Day, by boys only, who went around the village independent of each other with bundles of firewood. The boys would sing a carol and throw a piece of wood into the house; only then could they expect pennies as a reward. Girls took part in this custom at New Year.

Hemswell: When a pig was killed in a household, it was custom to make mince pies out of the meat, called minch pies.

Holton-le-Clay: The Passing Bell would be tolled when someone was dying because evil spirits dislike the sound. The spirits would divide, leaving a pathway for the departing soul to travel to Heaven.

Isle of Axholme: When a death occurred in a family that kept bees, black crepe was placed on the hive, otherwise the bees would leave in search of the departed, or die themselves.

Lincoln: On Sundays during the 1920s and '30s, the city held a dating ritual in the High Street. The Monkey Parade, also known as the Monkey Walk, saw young people don fine clothes and promenade, with men on one side and women on the other. Nods, smiles and winks often led to courting.

Stainton-le-Vale: Women went mumping on St Thomas' Day. They woke early and visited farmhouses, where they were given wheat. The women made the wheat into Frumenty, a porridge-like dish considered a delicacy. In the Isle of Axholme, old women went mumping for tea and bread.

LINCOLNSHIRE'S TAKE ON MEDICINAL REMEDIES

To ward off rheumatism, wear a mole's foot on a watch chain or carry it in a pocket.

To stop a nosebleed, suddenly drop a cold key down the afflicted's back.

Gargle with paraffin to cure diphtheria.

To get rid of a wart, rub a toad on it. The toad must be passed to someone else, who must hang it on a thorn bush. As the toad withers and dies, the wart will too.

FOLKLORE BY AREA

Boston: Inhabitants call the footpath between the river and Boston Stump tower 'Windy Corner', for there's a breeze even on still days. St Botolph had an encounter with the Devil on the footpath, and the Devil was given such a beating that he remains there now, panting from exhaustion.

Digby: If you see a white dog, you must not speak a word until you see a white horse.

Gainsborough: If a single lady takes the last piece of bread and butter from a plate, she will forever be a spinster.

Grayingham: When the head of a household dies, rooks will desert the rookery for a year.

Hemswell: When getting out of bed, put the right foot on the floor first, otherwise you will be bad-tempered all day.

Isle of Axholme: If a visitor leaves their gloves at your house, the visitor must, upon their return, first sit down and then put them on while standing up, otherwise the visitor will never come back.

Kirton-in-Lindsey: To break the habit of wetting the bed, give the child ground-up egg shell in milk or water. In Gunthorpe, the cure for bed-wetting is mouse pie.

Scawby: When bracken is down in July, it will be a harsh winter.

Willoughton: If your nose tickles, it's a sign you will be kissed, cursed or vexed, or you will shake hands with a fool.

Wilsford: If the sun shines at midday on Christmas Day, it will be a good year for apples.

LINCOLNSHIRE OMENS

It is considered good luck to: meet a sheep; carry coal in your pocket; for a black cat to cross your path; to meet someone with a squint; and to see a lot of magpies together. In Gainsborough, it's good luck if you can pass a half-crown between your two front teeth.

It is considered bad luck in Gainsborough to spill ink, pick up a flower that has been dropped, or place new shoes on a table. In Digby, removing your wedding ring means seven years' bad luck, as is dropping an umbrella, bringing May blossom into the house, and seeing a white horse (but to avert it, cross your fingers).

LEGENDS FROM DOWN THE YEARS

Cusset, who lived in Louth in the 1880s, was a wise man. People would travel to consult him. One man, from Holton-le-Clay, lost a gold watch. He sought Cusset's advice, and went home to the watch's exact spot.

Gainsborough is connected to the legend of Canute, the Danish king of England. To prove to flatterers that he did have limits to his power, Canute stood at the River Trent and waited for the spring equinox tidal wave that still travels along the river to this day. He commanded the wave to not wet him, but Canute was drenched, and he declared: 'Let all the world know that the power of the monarch is in vain... no one deserves the name of the King but He whose Will the Heavens, Earth and Sea do obey.'

The Lincoln Imp is one of many devil gargoyles found in Lincoln Cathedral, sitting atop a pillar above the Angel Choir. Two imps were brought on strong winds to see the newly built cathedral. The first was so amazed that its heart turned to stone and he became rooted to the ground. The other alighted on the shoulders of a witch, which flew the imp to its place on the pillar, where she turned it to stone.

King John lost his treasure in the Wash, while travelling north with his army. He misjudged the timing of high tide and had to abandon his treasure to escape the strong undercurrents and quicksand. After this, he went to Swineshead Abbey, where he was allegedly poisoned by monks. He died seven days later at Newark Castle.

Tom Hickathrift, who lived on marshland by the Wash, was a giant; aged 10, he was 6ft tall. Once a kind farmer offered his mother as much straw as Tom could carry to refill her mattress, so Tom returned with almost the entire field, such was his strength. Tom was eventually employed by a brewer to transport carts of beer 20 miles each day. Once, he decided to travel over land inhabited by an angry giant. Tom beheaded the giant using a cart wheel and axle, and was hailed a hero. There are many other versions of this legend.

Lincolnshire had a wild man of the woods who killed locals and livestock, but was overcome by Francis Tyrwhitt-Drake. A monument stands in Bigby's church to Sir Robert Tyrwhitt, depicting a hairy man lying across his feet. There is a wild man on the sign of the Tyrwhitt Arms, in South Ferriby.

In Grimsby, a carved wooden statue of a pipe-smoking Elizabethan, thought to be Sir Walter Raleigh, stood proudly atop Chapman's Hotel. At night, Sir Walter would climb down from his bird's-eye perch for a liaison with the statue of a lady on top of the Palace Theatre, in nearby Victoria Street.

IT'S WITCHCRAFT...

In 1618 Joan Flowers lived with her daughters Margaret and Phillipa, who were both in service at Belvoir Castle. Yellowbellies long suspected Joan had supernatural powers, and it came to a head when Margaret was dismissed from her job. At the same time, Joan was jilted because of gossip surrounding her.

Joan blamed the Earl and Countess of Rutland for both occurrences, so she and her daughters joined forces with Anne Baker, Joan Willimot and Ellen Green, who swore to take revenge on those who had wronged them. They made a pact with Satan, exchanging their souls for supernatural powers; Joan's came in the form of a black cat, Rutterkin.

Margaret, who had many male admirers among the staff at Belvoir, was sent back to the castle and easily gained entrance. She stole wool from the bed of the earl and countess, a pair of the countess's gloves, gloves belonging to the couple's young sons, Lord Henry and Lord Francis Roos, and their daughter Katherine's handkerchief.

To kill Henry, ringleader Joan rubbed his glove on Rutterkin's back and pricked it with pins; Henry did indeed die in agony, although the exact cause of his illness is not recorded. The witch also cast spells on his brother Francis's glove and buried it in a dung heap so the child would waste and rot away. Francis died from a disease that caused him to lose weight.

Katherine did not die in infancy like her brothers, but suffered mysterious illnesses and fits. Joan had apparently tried to rub Katherine's glove on Rutterkin's back, but the cat did not allow it.

Joan's final act against the family was to boil the wool from the earl and countess's bed in a pot containing cockerel's blood and feathers to make the couple sterile. They had no more children.

The gang's activities were notorious throughout Lincolnshire, Leicestershire and Rutland, particularly in Grantham. They enjoyed boasting of their successful dabbles in the occult, and their story of revenge on the earl and countess made its way back to the castle.

They were soon interrogated and although they accused each other, their statements led not only to a charge of causing the deaths of the earl's sons, but also the death of a child called Anne Stannidge. It was alleged that they burned her hair and nail parings while nursing her.

Ellen Green was alleged to have killed a baker because he called her a witch, and was accused of killing Ann Daws because she had called Ellen names.

The gang as a whole were accused of holding coven meetings at night on Blackborrow Hill and near Grantham, and were sent to trial at Lincoln Castle.

On the journey, Joan Flowers asked for a piece of bread, declaring, 'Should I not be telling the truth, may this bread choke me'. She swallowed the bread, fell to the floor and died. The remaining witches were kept in prison prior to their trial, where Margaret Flowers said four devils – one in the form of Rutterkin and another with a black head like an ape – appeared to her one midnight.

These stories strengthened the case against the gang and, on 11 March 1618, they were found guilty of murder and executed in Lincoln. Today, we have a reminder of their reign of terror. A monument in the church at Bottesford, Leicestershire, bears the inscription: 'In 1608, he [6th Earl of Rutland] married Cecilia Hungerford, by whom he had two sons, both of whom died in their infancy by wicked practice and sorcery.'

BEWARE OF HARES AND RATS

Dorrington: An old woman here could transform into a rat. One night she chose to confront a local on his way home from the pub. Annoyed, he stood on the rat's tail and kicked it, and the creature ran off. The next day, villagers spotted blood on the path of the old woman's cottage. Alarmed, they knocked on the door and broke in to find her battered, bloody and bruised.

Rowston: Rowston's witch enjoyed turning into a hare to cause mayhem. She was shot and escaped to her cottage, but was found the next day in her human form, shot to pieces.

South Kyme: Villagers were reputed to be gossipers who could not keep secrets. Every time a group gathered to chat, a rat would appear and listen to their conversations. One day, workmen on a farm were having lunch when they noticed the rodent, listening to them, so one of the men struck it across the back with a hay fork. The rat escaped and later on, an elderly female villager was found with back and leg injuries.

Tetford: An old lady here could turn herself into a hare at will, playing havoc with crops and other animals in the village. One farmer grew tired of the witch's pranks and shot the hare's feet. The following morning, the old woman was found dead in her bed – with her hands and feet missing.

A SPELL TO SEE YOUR FUTURE HUSBAND

On Halloween, light a candle and stick pins in it. With each pin, a ditty must be said (the passage of time has lost the wording but each pin relates to a particular man). The candle will burn through each pin until stopping at the right man, and a door will open and the man will appear.

8

LINCOLNSHIRE AT WAR

1141: THE FIRST BATTLE OF LINCOLN

Stephen of Blois, the grandson of William the Conqueror, took the throne upon Henry I's death, usurping his mother, Matilda, who was heir to the kingdom.

A civil war, known as The Anarchy, lasted for most of Stephen's reign. Lincoln was besieged by Stephen, who tried to capture the castle, recently taken by Ranulf of Chester.

He supported neither Stephen or Matilda, but joined with his father-in-law, Robert of Gloucester (Matilda's illegitimate half-brother), to attack.

Stephen, surrounded, fought bravely, according to accounts, with a battle-axe and then a sword when the axe broke. A stone was thrown at his head and he was dragged to the ground. His men fled and it is understood that several hundred were captured and killed in Lincoln.

Stephen was transported to Bristol and kept in the castle there; he was eventually released after Robert of Gloucester was captured.

The conflict continued until 1153; Stephen reigned until his death in 1154, and he was succeeded by Henry II, Matilda's son.

CROMWELL IN ARMS

A major battle was fought at Winceby in October 1643 – probably Lincolnshire's most famous skirmish of the Civil War.

The Royalist garrison based at Bolingbroke Castle was under siege by Parliamentarians, and 200 men were killed as the castle was destroyed.

Royalist commander Sir Ingram Hopton was killed and given a military funeral in Horncastle. He was buried in St Mary's Church there, at Cromwell's express orders. Legend has it that Sir Ingram was decapitated, which frightened his horse so much that it galloped away, carrying his master's headless body in the saddle.

RAF'S YOUNG STAR AND MORE AWARD-WINNERS

Eighteen-year-old John Hannah was the youngest man in the RAF to receive the Victoria Cross.

John was a wireless operator and air gunner in one of 83 Squadron's Hampdens, from RAF Scampton, which were attacking barges in Antwerp on 15 September 1940.

His aircraft was shot down, and John fought the fire with extinguishers and his bare hands to put it out, allowing the pilot to return safely back to Lincolnshire.

The *Chandos* (GY 1290) acted as an auxiliary patrol vessel for the Admiralty and returned to fishing in January 1940, but was targeted on 31 March that year by a German plane as she voyaged through a snow squall in the North Sea.

Skipper John Upton was killed when gunfire struck the wheelhouse. Eighteen-year-old trimmer Clifford Rawlins was injured but got hold of the trawler's Lewis gun and fired back at the aircraft.

The vessel returned home to Grimsby and later, back at sea, the wreckage of an enemy plane was caught in its nets.

Clifford was awarded the British Empire Medal and the Lloyds War Medal for his courage.

A fearless Keelby bomber pilot who survived being shot down over the sea was presented with the Distinguished Flying Cross by King George VI at Buckingham Palace in 1944. Flying Officer George Bertram Willerton, born in Keelby in 1917, was awarded four other medals for his courage. The citation read:

> Flying Officer Willerton was captain of a Liberator aircraft set on fire when attacked by five Junker 88s while on an anti-submarine patrol over the Bay of Biscay. The aircraft was forced down on to the sea but, although underwater, Flying Officer Willerton managed to crawl through a side window, swim to a floating dinghy and, in a dazed condition, pulled aboard two members of his crew with him, one severely wounded. Without first aid equipment, he dressed his companion's wounds as well as he could and then paddled the dinghy for six days before being rescued.

That wasn't his only lucky escape. On 27 January 1942, while on a patrol over northern France, his plane was hit by anti-aircraft fire and he was forced to fly back to England on one engine. When over land, he parachuted out of the stricken plane. He noted in his log book: 'Landed on Dartmoor. Landed heavily, resulting in black eye.'

Essex lad John Cornwall, known as Jack, joined the Royal Navy on HMS *Chester* as part of the gun crew.

During the Battle of Jutland, he was the only survivor of his team when the ship was hit by German shells. Severely injured, he remained at his post.

The ship sailed for Immingham for repairs and Jack was taken to Grimsby General Hospital, where he sadly died from his injuries before his mother could make the journey to him.

Jack was posthumously awarded the Victoria Cross in November 1916 – at 16, he was one of Britain's youngest recipients.

Flying Officer Leslie Manser (20) was returning to RAF Skellingthorpe from a bombing raid on Cologne in May 1942 when his Manchester Bomber was targeted by anti-aircraft fire.

When the plane was over Belgian airspace, he ordered his crew to bail out, refusing to parachute himself so he could remain at the controls. The plane went down and FO Manser died. He was posthumously awarded the Victoria Cross.

Flight Lieutenant Alistair Learoyd (27) piloted a Hampden of 49 Squadron on a raid to blow up an aqueduct over the River Ems in Germany in August 1940.

His Hampden was picked out by searchlights and hit by two shells and several bullets. Undeterred, Learoyd flew slowly back to base at RAF Scampton, Lincoln. To save his crew and the plane, he circled the base for two hours until dawn broke, and landed safely.

His bravery was rewarded with a Victoria Cross.

Flight Lieutenant Learoyd commanded 83 Squadron at Scampton for a short while before joining 44 Squadron at RAF Waddington, flying on the famous Augsburg raid.

'Learoyd' remains as one of the names of the living quarters near the entrance to RAF Scampton.

SOME GRIMSBY VESSELS LOST DURING THE SECOND WORLD WAR

Dinorah	Leonora
Elmira	Mistletoe
Fortuna	Ontario
Greynight	Pride of the Humber
Lynx II	Slasher

BAND OF BROTHERS: THE BEECHEY BOYS

The Beechey Boys were eight Lincolnshire brothers who went to war – only three returned.

The family lived in Friesthorpe with Snarford, where their father, the Reverend Prince William Thomas Beechey, was rector. They moved to Avondale Street in Lincoln when he became ill with cancer.

Sergeant Barnard Reeve Beechey was born in 1877 and was a deputy headmaster in Dorchester. He was in the 2nd Battalion of the Lincolnshire Regiment, and the eldest of the brothers to die in action on 5 September 1915, aged 38, at the Battle of Loos.

Private Charles Reeve Beechey, of the 25th Battalion of the Royal Fusiliers, was born in 1878 and before the war was a schoolmaster at Stamford School. He died from wounds on 10 October 1917, aged 39, in East Africa.

Second Lieutenant Frank Collett Reeve Beechey was a schoolmaster at Hornsea and Horsham before joining De Aston School, Market Rasen. He left there for a position at the Lincoln Choir School when he joined the 15th Battalion of the East Yorkshire Regiment. He died on 14 November 1916, aged 30, having been wounded by a Somme shell.

Lance Corporal Harold Reeve Beechey, born in 1891, was a pupil at De Aston School and emigrated aged 22 to Australia. He joined the 48th Battalion of the Australian Infantry of the Australian Air Force and was killed by a bomb in Bullecourt, France, on 10 April 1917, aged 26. During service, he had been invalided twice and wounded once.

Rifleman Leonard Reeve Beechey, born 1881, became a railway clerk after studying at Christ's Hospital School in Lincoln and Stamford School. A member of the 18th (County of London) Battalion, London Regiment (London Irish Rifles), he was gassed and wounded at Bourlon Wood and died of his wounds, aged 36, on 29 December 1917.

Their mother Amy was presented to King George V and Queen Mary in April 1818, who commended her for her sacrifice. She replied, 'It was no sacrifice, Ma'am. I did not give them willingly.'

The only other known family to have lost five sons in the First World War is the Souls of Gloucestershire.

LINCOLNSHIRE'S THANKFUL VILLAGES

Lincolnshire has four recorded 'Thankful Villages'. The phrase was coined by travel writer Arthur Mee to describe the very few areas that did not suffer fatalities during the First World War. There are fifty-two in England overall.

In Lincolnshire, they are Flixborough, High Toynton, Bigby and Minting. Flixborough and High Toynton are doubly thankful, as every man who went to fight from both the First and Second World Wars returned.

BOYS DETERMINED TO BE MEN

Albert Waddingham was born in 1900 in Burton-upon-Stather, the son of a brickyard worker, and was an errand boy before joining the Royal Navy in 1915, aged 15. He was posted to the *Queen Mary* and four days later was in action at the Battle of Jutland.

Albert was among 1,266 men who died when a magazine explosion blew up the ship – just ten days after his 16th birthday.

Although men were not allowed to enlist until they were 19, many lied about their age to help their country, including the following Lincolnshire lads:

George Ernest Lancaster signed up to the Army aged 16. He was badly wounded in the leg but came through the war to work for the Post Office in Gainsborough. He served with the Home Guard during the Second World War and died in Gainsborough in 1971.

Alfred Newbury was born in a caravan in Monks Road, Lincoln, on Christmas Eve 1897. His parents settled in the city and at 16, Alfred joined the 1st Battalion of the Lincolnshire Regiment. He served on the Western Front, and on 16 June 1915 was wounded at Hooge, Flanders. He died four days later in Calais.

Herbert Thomas Elliott was born in November 1898 and educated in Lincoln. He became a member of the 1/4th Battalion of the Lincolnshire Regiment in August 1914, aged 15. He saw action on the Front and died of wounds received on the first day of the Battle of the Somme.

A LOST LANCASTER

A military accident in Lincolnshire caused the death of the only woman ever to perish in a Lancaster.

Taniya Whittall was a pilot in the Air Transport Auxiliary (ATA), which was tasked with delivering aircraft to RAF airfields. Its most famous pilot was Amy Johnson, Hull's aviation pioneer.

Taniya, the daughter of a retired Indian Army officer from East Sussex, was determined to be a pilot, and succeeded in her ambition. She came to Lincolnshire in April 1944, possibly to deliver a Spitfire to RAF Kirton Lindsey or the airfield at Hibaldstow, both of which were Spitfire training grounds.

She stayed overnight at the No.1 Lancaster Finishing School, at RAF Hemswell. It was common for passengers to be invited on test flights, and it's thought that this is why she was one of nine people who died on board a Lancaster when it crashed near Caistor's small RAF airfield on 8 April.

An inquest heard that the plane was flying low when the engine spluttered and an explosion occurred. It was the only Lancaster lost from the Finishing School, and was so badly damaged that the cause of the accident could not be determined. Taniya's ATA cap, powder compact and pilot's licence were recovered from the wreckage. She was one of twenty ATA pilots killed during the Second World War.

GIBBON'S GULLEY: AN ACCIDENTAL LANDMARK

Gibbons' Gulley was accidentally created on 10 April 1944.

Kirmington then was the home of 166 Squadron, and their Lancasters were to be part of a major 1 Group attack on railway yards in Aulnoyne, France. Four aircraft had already taken off when it came to the turn of the F-Fox, which was laden with fourteen 1,000lb bombs.

Halfway down the runway a tyre burst and despite the efforts of the pilot, Sergeant Gibbons, the aeroplane's undercarriage caught fire. The crew ran and it exploded, shattering every window within a mile's radius of the airfield and leaving a crater in the main runway measuring 50ft wide and 15ft deep.

By the following morning, more than 100 men were working flat out to move 500 tons of earth to fill the crater. By 12.30 p.m. the hole had been filled and at 8 p.m. Lancasters were again taking off from Kirmington, this time for a raid on Aachen.

A month later, the patched-up hole began to subside and Kirmington was closed for several days while repairs were carried out. When the airfield re-opened as the region's airport in 1974, there was still a noticeable dip in the runway.

GRIMSBY'S BLOODY THURSDAY

On 27 February 1941, a raid carried out by a lone Dornier aircraft – lasting only a few minutes – killed eleven people and injured twenty-seven.

The plane emerged from low cloud over Humberston and used a machine gun over Toll Bar School, and the number 8 bus had a narrow escape. It dropped a stick of bombs and continued to fire over Grimsby, along Cleethorpe Road. It then gunned traffic in Scartho Road and Louth Road before leaving.

Two children died as they made their way home from school, and others died when The Oberon, a popular watering hole for dockers, collapsed because a neighbouring fruit stall had been struck by a bomb.

KILLED IN ACTION: OUR MEN REMEMBERED

Sergeant John Chafer, of the 1st Battalion of the Lincolnshire Regiment, was the first man from Immingham to die in the First World War. John – who enlisted using the first name Herbert – lived in Waterworks Street with his wife and two children and was a police constable on Immingham Docks before he signed up. He was killed in action on 27 October 1914.

Charles Haw was born in June 1924 and lived in New Holland, moving later to Battery Street in Immingham, where he worked for the LNER. He joined the Royal Marines and in June 1942 went into the Holding Battalion before applying for the Commandos. He served in Akyab, an island off the coast of Burma, with No.44 Royal Marine Commandos. On 6 January 1945 he died from accidental gunshot wounds received in the barracks at Akyab.

A Grimsby Chum killed in action was 22-year-old Private Harry Boulton. He was born in Thorganby and lived in Immingham. A talented artist, he was employed at Hewson's Farm, in North Cotes, before joining the Chums in November 1915. He was posted to France in June the following year but was invalided home three months later following an operation. Undeterred, he returned to France in January 1917, dying on 9 April 1917 when the Chums were involved in the start of the Arras offensive. His body was never recovered.

Leading Stoker Ernest Potter, aged 22, was swept overboard on 26 May 1941. He was born in Immingham and worked as an errand boy and grocery assistant in Alderman Tate's shop in Grimsby. Ernest joined the Royal Navy in 1937 and was sent to serve on the destroyer HMS *Sikh* during the war. While on Christmas leave in 1940, he married his Grimsby sweetheart Molly. They had a short honeymoon – and Molly never saw him again. On 21 May 1941, the vessel was ordered to search for the German battleship *Bismarck* in the Atlantic. Ernest was swept overboard by a giant wave one day before the *Bismarck* was sunk.

Norman Jacobson, from Grimsby, became one of the youngest aviators to die in the Battle of Britain. He was 18 years old when he joined the RAF in 1940, becoming an operator with 29 Squadron. On 25 August, he was one of a three-strong crew on a Blenheim sent to investigate sightings of an intruder over the Wash. The plane took off... and was never heard of again. Two days later, Norman's body was found in the sea by an armed Grimsby trawler, *The Alfredian*, being skippered by John Vincent, a veteran of Shackleton's 1914 Antarctic expedition. Not realising Norman's parents were in Grimsby, the crew buried him at sea.

Aubrey Edward Glew was born in 1891 at South Kelsey Hall. He was educated at De Aston in Market Rasen from 1903 to 1905, and joined the Lincolnshire Yeomanry before joining the Royal Flying Corps. In 1916, he was sent to France with the No. 24 Squadron, and within his first six weeks at the Western Front, shot down four enemy aircraft. On 8 September 1916, he was flying over German lines when his engine burst into flames. He controlled the descent to about 500ft but crashed. He was 25 years old. His mother received the news of his death as she was reading a letter from Aubrey, telling her how excited he was about being home on leave in a few days.

Three Lincolnshire men were on board HMS *Hampshire* when it set off from the Orkneys on 5 June 1916 to Russia, with War Minister Lord Kitchener on board. Just 1.5 miles off land, there was a storm and an explosion was heard in the ship's port side. The rough seas meant the lifeboats could not be launched, and the ship sank within fifteen minutes. Of 662 men on board, 650 perished, including Lord Kitchener. One of the youngest who died was 17-year-old Edgar Purnell, from Ruskington in Lincolnshire. Able Seaman Edward Cecil George and Stoker Wilfred Chambers Lowe, both from Lincoln, also lost their lives.

William Henry Shaw, of Lincoln, was just 16 years old when he died on board HMS *Hawke*. On 15 October 1914 it was patrolling the North Sea when it was hit by an enemy torpedo. The ship sank within a few minutes, and only seventy men survived; the captain, twenty-six officers and 497 men perished. William was from a poor family and worked as an errand boy to add to his labourer father's wages. He joined the Royal Navy in September 1913.

MEETING A LEGEND

An encounter with Guy Gibson – just before he became famous – was recorded by local historian Kit Lawie, from East Keal.

Her father, a shepherd in the Home Guard, found three airmen in flying gear hiding behind trees near the family home.

He assumed they were crashed Germans and called for them to come out of their hiding place. To his surprise, they replied that they were English and asked where they were. They explained that they'd been taken in a covered lorry from Woodhall Spa aerodrome as part of an exercise and dumped in the middle of nowhere; their challenge was to return to base without being caught by the police or the Home Guard.

They had spent the night under a hedge, so Kit's father invited them home for breakfast. Kit recalled them walking into the house but starting when they saw her brother in his Home Guard uniform. Once they realised it wasn't a trap, they ate a hearty meal and introduced themselves. One of the men was named Temple, whom the others called 'Shirley', and another said, 'I'm Guy Gibson.' As the family sent them safely on their way back to base through Claxby Pluckacre, one of them whispered to Kit's brother to keep an eye out, for their names would soon be known. How right they were: this meeting took place just six weeks before the legendary Dambusters raid. The attack was immortalised on film, with Richard Todd starring as Gibson in a movie filmed at RAF Scampton.

BRIEF HISTORIES OF
SOME WARTIME STATIONS

RAF Waddington was established in 1916 as a training station and rebuilt in the 1930s to become a bomber base during the war. It reverted to training and in 1953 it was renovated to accommodate Vulcan bombers. The first operational Vulcan squadron, No. 83, was established at Waddington in 1957. By 1961, there were three squadrons. When Vulcans were phased out in 1984, Waddington became home to the Nimrod Airborne Early Warning Project and then in 1986 to the Airborne Warfare and Control System.

North Cotes Airfield was built during the First World War and closed in March 1919, being re-opened as a permanent airfield in 1934. During the Second World War, it was under Coastal Command's Control, responsible for bombing enemy shipping. In the 1950s it became the first missile site for Fighter Command, housing surface-to-air Bloodhound missiles. It closed in 1971, opening five years on to house missiles withdrawn from Singapore and Cyprus. It was operational until the 1990s, when it was sold and is now a private airfield.

The No. 57 and No. 630 squadrons were housed at East Kirkby Airfield, constructed specifically for the Second World War during 1942 and 1943. It remained operational until July 1948 and lay unoccupied until 1952, when it became a USAF airbase. To accommodate the B-47 bombers, one of the runways was extended, but it was actually used for Dakotas instead. The airfield was left to its own devices once more in 1958, and the land returned to agriculture. An aviation museum now occupies the site.

RAF Coningsby in 1940 had a single grass runway which could not cope with heavy bombers. It reopened in 1943 with concrete runways and became the base for squadrons of Lancasters until the end of the war. It was modernised between 1954 and 1956, and from 1962 Vulcans were based there. In 1966 it became the first base for the Phantom fighter-bombers and also trained Phantom crews. It then went on to house Tornado F3s and the Battle of Britain Memorial Flight.

The Royal Air Force Cadet College at Cranwell was opened following a proposal by Winston Churchill. Group Captain Douglas Bader was one of its graduates, in 1930. In 1942, a British aircraft crashed onto the roof of the college. All the crew were killed and the crash started a major fire.

RAF Scampton, which first came into being under the name of Brittlely in 1916, has been at the forefront of aviation technology.

It was first a Searchlight Defence Unit, but as the First World War continued, the station transformed into an Operational Training Unit. When the conflict came to an end in 1918, the station was run down and by the 1920s the land had been returned to agricultural use.

A decade later, when war threatened once more, Scampton became a permanent RAF base and was brought back into use in 1936. In later years the station became home to the Red Arrows, meaning it will forever be in Lincolnshire's history books.

HOLY COW!

As a young lad, Bob Riddington, of Willoughby, was a local fire and plane spotter, and would often spend the night inside a wooden lambing hut, on wheels, in the middle of a field. One night, an air-raid siren sounded at Alford and he could see searchlights. After about an hour, the hut began to rock back and forth. Frightened, he eventually plucked up the courage to look outside – to find an old cow rubbing its behind against the hut.

WHAT A DUMMY:
LINCOLNSHIRE'S DECOYS

In 1939 and 1940, decoy aerodromes were set up to distract German bombers from nearby operational airfields. Known as K sites, there was a dummy drome at Hagnaby, serving RAF Coningsby. The first personnel arrived in February 1940, and one of those was Corporal Geoff Hall, who had received training in constructing and dismantling dozens of dummy aircraft, made to scale at Shepperton Film Studios out of three-ply and cardboard.

The aerodrome was equipped with props including old ambulances and a fire tender, all of which had to be moved about so it looked operational; even mock runways were lit up with flares when the enemy approached.

The crew of about thirty-five lived on site twenty-four hours a day. When an air-raid warning came from RAF Coningsby, they would power a generator, start operating searchlights, and light the flare path and imitation landing lights. One night there were five explosions when a German plane bombed a decoy, and the crew spent the next day filling in craters so they were not discovered.

Corporal Hall recalled how the kindly Maxwell family, who lived at Hagnaby Priory, would welcome crewmen into their home for warmth and food. The Barnes, who lived in nearby farm cottages, would do the airmen's laundry. Because much of their work was at night, the men would go to the cinema in the day or roller-skating in Boston.

Corporal Doug Feary was posted for just one day at RAF Coningsby before being deployed to Hagnaby.

He remembered how the fake planes were mounted on steel pipes, and during those first patrols the only weapons they had were pick-axe handles. There was no toilet either; only a hole in the ground under a crab apple tree. The Red Lion, in nearby Stickford, would let them visit to bathe.

One evening, the crew heard thuds but not explosions. At first light, they discovered that the Germans had dropped wooden bombs on the aerodrome and that the game was up for Hagnaby's dummy drome. It was operational from March 1940 to June 1941. Other decoy airfields for Coningsby were at Frithville and Sibsey. RAF Manby's was at Mablethorpe.

A FESTIVE PROBLEM TO SOLVE

In 1899, the Post Office in the Lincolnshire Fens had a problem.

Queen Victoria decreed that mail from men fighting in the Boer War must be delivered in time for Christmas, and this had left officials scratching their heads.

It meant a Christmas Day delivery, but trains were not running… so their solution was to deliver the mail from Lincoln to the village of New York and other places inbetween, deep in the countryside, by car.

It's thought to be the first instance of a car being used to deliver mail in the provinces, maybe even in the entire country.

At 7.40 a.m. on Christmas Day, the car set off with half a ton of mail, reaching Washingborough in thirteen minutes. It travelled to Heightington Fen and was then ferried over the River Withal to Fiskerton. Deliveries at various locations continued, and the car reached New York at 11.20 a.m., having made a 34-mile journey. On the return journey to Lincoln, the car collected mail from Tattershall, Coningsby, Tattershall Bridge and Billinghay, reaching the Post Office in the city at 6.45 p.m. – just in time for the night mail!

SOME WARTIME FACTS

Lord Louis Mountbatten used the County Hotel in Immingham as his headquarters briefly during the Second World War, while HMS *Kelly* was being repaired. His vessel had been damaged by the enemy, and was eventually lost off Crete in 1941.

Field Marshall Sir William Robertson, who was born in January 1860 in Welbourn, was the first man ever to serve in all ranks of the British Army. He joined the service as a private at the age of 17, serving in India and the Boer War, and died in 1933.

When it became apparent that the Germans would invade Norway, King Haakon and his Norwegian Navy security officers were sent to safety… in Ingoldmells. His Majesty stayed at The Ace of Spades.

Grimsby and Plymouth are the only locations in Britain where anti-personnel bombs – or butterfly bombs – were dropped by the enemy during the Second World War. This occurred in Grimsby on 13 and 14 June 1943, and ninety-nine people died.

The Chain Home Radar Site, at Stenigot, was one of twenty stations in the world's first air defence radar system. It began operations in 1939 and is now disused. Four giant dishes, two facing Kent and two facing Northumberland, still visible today, were part of a system carrying air defence radar data and communications between NATO sites. They were built in about 1960 and taken out of service in 1992.

In August 1915, tentative steps towards military history were taken in Lincoln.

There was widespread horror at the number of casualties incurred through the stalemate at No Man's Land, and the task of ending the violence fell to the Admiralty Landships Committee. They were told to come up with a prototype for an armoured vehicle robust enough to cross trenches, travel through barbed wire, and be able to attack.

The First Lord of the Admiralty, Winston Churchill, had already mooted an idea of armed men inside a vehicle on caterpillar tractors.

The idea was finalised at an inaugural meeting at The White Hart, in Lincoln's Bailgate, and the first steps to make such a vehicle began at William Foster's engineering works.

To ensure the plan remained secret, the workforce there were told they were making 'water-carriers for Mesopotamia'.

The vehicles were soon referred to as tanks (as a security measure to conceal their purpose) – the first to be built for the British Army in the First World War.

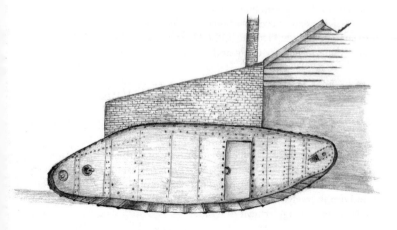

9

ROYALTY, RELIGION AND POLITICS

LINCOLNSHIRE'S ONLY KING

Henry IV was born at Bolingbroke Castle in 1367 – the only king known to have been born in Lincolnshire.

Aged 10, he became a Knight of the Garter under Edward III and carried a sword at Richard II's coronation. He remained at Bolingbroke until 1395, when he joined the council appointed to rule England while Richard II was in Ireland.

In 1397, he became the Duke of Hereford, but the following year quarrelled with the Duke of Norfolk and was banished. In 1399, the banishment was made permanent and his estates were confiscated. But Henry did not accept this: in July, he landed near Withernsea and gathered a large following. The King was captured and Henry demanded his rightful inheritance.

The King renounced the crown and Henry was chosen by Parliament to succeed him, in October 1399. Henry died in March 1413 and was buried at Canterbury Cathedral.

THE KING'S HANGOVER

Was William III worse for wear when he visited Lincoln Cathedral in 1695?

According to records, he brought provisions with him but ate nothing. This could be because William was suffering from the effects of merry-making. He had previously been in Belton and got 'exceedingly merry, and drank freely, which was the occasion when he came to Lincoln he could take but a porringer of milk'.

QUEEN ELEANOR'S CROSSES

On 4 December 1290, a journey began which has been marked ever since.

Eleanor of Castile, King Edward I's Queen, died at Harby, near Lincoln, on 29 November after wasting away from fever. Her body was taken to St Catharine's Priory in the city to be embalmed.

Her viscera was sent to the Angel Choir of Lincoln Cathedral for burial. An altar-tomb was erected under the east window, but this was destroyed in the Civil War in 1644.

The King left the priory in procession with his wife's body, taking twelve days to reach Westminster Abbey. He decreed that memorial crosses – known as Eleanor crosses – should be erected at the twelve places where the funeral procession stopped overnight, Lincoln being the first.

The crosses were originally wooden but later constructed of stone. At Westminster, Queen Eleanor was buried at the feet of her father-in-law, King Henry III. Her heart was buried at Blackfriars.

A RUSSIAN PRINCE IN LINCOLNSHIRE

Prince Yuri (Yurka) Nikolaievitch Galitzine was born in February 1919 in Japan as his parents were returning to the UK from America, where they stayed following the fall of the Russian monarchy.

He was the eldest son of Prince Nicholas Alexandrovitch Galitzine, who in 1916 was appointed Assistant Military Attache in the Imperial Russian Embassy in London. His mother, Emma Lilian Fawcett-Hodgson, came from a Westmoreland farming family.

For a time, the family lived in France and Austria before settling in England. Aged 11, Prince Yuri went to school in Sussex and learned English, going on to have an esteemed career in public relations. Married four times with five children, he chose to live in south Lincolnshire. The Prince passed away in 2002.

A QUEEN'S CONFIDANT

William Cecil was born in 1520 to a wealthy Lincolnshire landowner. When Elizabeth became Queen in 1558, he was made her Secretary of State. In 1572, he was appointed Lord Treasurer and became Baron Burleigh; Elizabeth regularly took his counsel. He fell ill in 1598 and the Queen would visit him. He died on 4 August and was buried at St Martin's Church, Stamford.

SPLASHING THE CASH ... IN PRISON

From August 1359 to March 1630, Somerton Castle was used as a jail for political prisoners, including King John II of France, who was guarded by forty-four men when he was escorted to Somerton for a six-month stint.

During his stay in Lincolnshire, he enjoyed a luxurious lifestyle: he lavished lots of cash on items of jewellery, as well as silver dishes and cups.

TWO OXFORD INSTITUTIONS THAT WOULDN'T EXIST

Richard Foxe was principal Secretary of State and Lord Privy Seal when Henry VII came to the throne.

Born in Ropsley in 1448, he was made Bishop of Exeter in 1487 and baptised the future King Henry VIII in 1491.

He was held in high esteem by the King and was, in fact, made an executor of the King's will.

Foxe established Corpus Christi College, Oxford, in 1515 and built Grantham's grammar school. For ten years before he died in 1528, he was blind. He was buried at Winchester Cathedral.

William Waynflete was born in Wainfleet in about 1395. He was ordained at Spalding in 1420 and soon after Eton was founded by Henry VI, William was made its provost.

In 1447, he was made Bishop of Winchester and founded Magdalen College, Oxford, in 1448 for the study of theology and philosophy.

On 11 October 1456, he became Lord Chancellor. He died in 1486 and is also buried at Winchester Cathedral.

FOUR COLOURFUL CLERGYMEN

Back in the 1300s, it seems the Deans of Lincoln Cathedral were known for their notorious behaviour as much as their religious calling.

Dr John Sheppey was appointed in 1388. Records show he accepted bribes so misdeeds would go unpunished, used insulting language and wasted Church resources on dances and theatrical performances. He also attended shows held on the commons outside the city, acted as umpire at wrestling matches and offered prizes to the top wrestlers!

When vicar choral – or professional cathedral singer – Thomas Parker decided to take leave of his post without permission, he got into trouble. In 1546 he was imprisoned at Le Wynde, Lincoln Cathedral's prison, by the Chapter for 'absenting himself' from the cathedral for three or four weeks without licence, leaving the vicarage and chantry 'unserved'.

Reverend Charles Joseph Edwards became rector of Ingoldmells in 1864, and although a good preacher, he was useless with money.

He requested that the parish vestry pay to replace a rotting fence around his cemetery. The cash-strapped vestry suggested it should be repaired instead. For some reason, the reverend ignored this and had iron railings installed – going back to the vestry to ask for the cash, which they refused.

The reverend ended up before local magistrates and was declared bankrupt with debts of £2,000 – including the cost of the fence – and assets of only £90.

He was sent to Lincoln Prison for ten years. When he was released, he returned to Ingoldmells and to the same position within the clergy.

Records do not reveal whether he became better at money management!

Austin Lee, who was brought up in Claxby, was an educated yet controversial man. He wanted to tackle apathy to religion, yet at the same time described bishops as 'timid little men'.

Following education and a curacy at Kew, followed by a stint as a Royal Navy chaplain, he returned to Claxby as vicar in 1944. Appointments in other areas followed, including time as rector of Willoughby with Sloothby, and in 1963 as curate in charge of Mumby; in his lifetime, he was also a chef, barman and schoolmaster.

His provocative views led him to become a feature writer for the *Daily Mirror* and the *Daily Mail*. Under the assumed names of John Austwick and Julian Calendar, he wrote detective stories and was a member of the Crime Writers' Association. He died in 1965.

SEVEN INTRIGUING CHURCHES

St Edith's Church in Grimoldby boasts twenty gargoyles. Some are water spouts but the rest are decorative in the style of winged dogs, a flying man, devils, animals, men and ladies. The oldest grave in the churchyard is that of John Dowle, who died in 1765, aged 106.

Glentham Church has a fourteenth-century stone sarcophagus lid, an effigy to Lady Anne Tournay. Every Good Friday, seven old maids washed it with well water, and each woman was paid 1s. Washing holy images was referred to as 'malgraen', which became corrupted to 'Molly Grime'. A child with a dirty face, therefore, is called 'Molly Grime'.

Great Ponton Church has a weathervane shaped like a violin. The original version was placed there in the seventeenth century, paid for by a fiddler who emigrated to America to find his fortune. Villagers, wishing him well in his venture, raised the money for his fare.

St Peter's in Markby is Lincolnshire's only church with a thatched roof. It was built in the seventeenth century from the ruins of Markby Priory.

Raithby Chapel, near Spilsby, has strong links with John Wesley and a connection with Methodism in South Africa. The movement was founded in the Cape area by British soldiers. In 1815, Yorkshire Methodist minister Reverend Barnabas Shaw attended a tea party at Raithby Hall with Wesley, and the hall's owner, Robert Carr Brackenbury, agreed to sponsor a mission to South Africa. Mr Shaw went to Cape Town in 1816, later settling at Lily Fountain in Kamiesberg. In 1834, he bought land in Somerset West, where he settled some emancipated slaves, and Methodism advanced.

Springthorpe Church possesses a maiden's garland. Bellringer Mary Hill died in 1814 when she became entangled in a rope and was pulled to the ceiling. She lost her grip and fell to the floor, hitting her head.

At her funeral, three white crowns of lilies and white gloves were carried to represent her chastity. One of these crowns is preserved at the church.

Winterton's churchyard has a tombstone made by the person it commemorates. The gentleman crafted his own stone before he died, using it as a table. He also made his coffin, utilising it as a cupboard for extra storage.

THE SAINT WHO ISN'T A SAINT

On 29 August 1255, the body of a 9-year-old boy was discovered in a well. Hugh had disappeared on 31 July, and it was suggested that Jews living in the city were responsible.

Hugh's friends claimed that Copin (or possibly Jopin), a local Jew, had imprisoned Hugh, torturing and crucifying him. His body had been buried but expelled by the earth, so he was thrown into the well.

Copin was arrested and, under torture, admitted killing the child but implicated the entire Jewish community before he was executed.

Soon, miracles were attributed to Hugh, and the boy became one of the youngest individual candidates for sainthood, with 27 July unofficially made his feast day.

Although he was never officially canonised, he is known as Little Saint Hugh of Lincoln. He is one of the best-known blood libel saints: generally, children whose deaths were interpreted as sacrifices committed by Jews.

Pilgrims flocked to the city up to the early twentieth century. Chaucer's *Canterbury Tales* makes reference to Hugh of Lincoln in *The Prioress's Tale*.

In 1975, folk-rock group Steeleye Span recorded 'Little Sir Hugh' on the album *Commoners Crown*.

FROM LITTLE TO BIG ST HUGH

St Hugh of Lincoln was a premier bishop in the kingdom. He was canonised in 1220, twenty years after his death, becoming the best-known British saint after murdered Thomas Becket.

The east end of the cathedral was extended to provide more space for ever-growing numbers of pilgrims. In October 1280, enough of the area known as the Angel Choir had been completed for a translation ceremony to re-site St Hugh's remains, which was witnessed by King Edward I and Queen Eleanor.

His shrine was located east of the choir screens, raised and surrounded by railings. It was destroyed during the Reformation but in about 1330 a new shrine was created for the relic of his head.

Hugh is the patron saint of sick children, sick people, shoemakers and swans.

'CAN ANY GOOD COME OUT OF CROWLE?': A BRIEF HISTORY OF JOHN WESLEY

John Wesley, a co-founder of the Methodist Church, was the second surviving son of nineteen children, born in June 1703 to Susannah and Samuel, the vicar of South Ormsby and later Epworth.

In Epworth, they were subjected to hostility from residents whom, in February 1709, set fire to the rectory. Samuel rescued his children and their nurse, while Susannah escaped alone.

They thought everyone was safe, until they realised 5-year-old John was still asleep inside. The noise of burning thatch woke him and he escaped through a window. This had a lasting effect on John, who believed God had chosen him for a great purpose.

When he was 10, he was educated in London for six years. It was during this time that his family in Epworth were plagued by supernatural happenings. John's sister Nancy was lifted up in the air before her sisters and servants. Samuel, who did not believe in such things, was pushed violently by unseen hands. The family eventually grew accustomed to the presence, nicknamed Old Jeffrey, and when

John returned from school an educated 17 year old, he investigated but the mystery was never solved.

He studied at Oxford, where he began writing journals, and was ordained in 1725.

In March the following year, John was made a Fellow of Lincoln College and by 1729 was a tutor at Lincoln, helping his brother Charles with his own studies.

Charles was dissatisfied with religious life and became the focal point of the Holy Club, whose members aimed to become better Christians.

John got involved too and the club later changed its name to Methodists, because of the methods they subscribed to. One enthusiast was George Whitefield, who later went on to lead Methodists in America. From these beginnings, Methodism was born.

For years, John kept meticulous diaries. In August 1759, he preached at Gainsborough Old Hall, by invitation of owner Sir Nevil Hickman, and wrote: 'At two o'clock it was filled with a rude, wild multitude... Yet all but two or three gentlemen were attentive while I enforced our Lord's words.' In 1748 he preached at Crowle to the wildest congregation he ever experienced, noting, 'Can any good come out of Crowle?'

In June 1786 at Belton, while Wesley was preaching, three young children became distracted. One fell into a well, and the others too while trying to rescue their friend. The youngest tragically died. Wesley died in March 1791. His last words were, 'Best of all, God is with us.'

MAGIC AGAINST THE QUEEN: JOHN DEE

Alchemist and philosopher Dr John Dee – advisor to the Crown on astrological events – was rector of Long Leadenham from 1566 until he died in either 1608 or 1609.

He was an eminent scientist and mathematician, learned in the occult and esoteric, but lost favour when Queen Mary came to the throne.

He was jailed in 1555 for using enchantments against the Queen, but was reinstated when Queen Elizabeth I was crowned in 1558.

THE SALVATION ARMY'S CAISTOR ROOTS

William Booth, the Salvation Army founder, spent time in Lincolnshire – and credits the county for inspiring him.

Aged 23, he became minister of the Spalding circuit of the Wesleyan Reform Movement. He preached in the Fenlands and in December 1853 was asked to lead a crusade in Caistor.

He visited there three times before becoming a travelling evangelist with the New Connexion. He married Catherine Mumford, who stayed in Caistor while expecting their first child. The couple's passion for simple principles saw them establish the Christian Mission in 1865, later renamed the Salvation Army, with William as its general.

General Booth returned to Caistor in 1905, flags and bunting adorning the high street. He said it was in Caistor that he began work on the movement which meant so much to him.

THE 106-YEAR-OLD SAINT

Gilbert of Sempringham, the son of a Norman knight who came to England with William the Conqueror, was born in about 1085.

He was shunned for a deformity, so went to France. When he returned to England in 1123, his father gave him the livings of Sempringham and Torrington.

Gilbert gave the revenue to the poor and taught at free schools, establishing the priory of Sempringham in 1135. The Order of the Gilbertines was approved and priories were established in Alvingham, North Ormsby, Six Hills, West Torrington and Lincoln.

Gilbert supposedly died aged 106, when there were twenty-six Gilbertine houses in England. He was canonised in 1202 and St Gilbert's feast day is celebrated on 4 February.

THE MAN BEHIND THE SAMARITANS

Edward Chad Varah – named after the founder of Barton-upon-Humber's St Peter's Church – was born at Barton Rectory on 12 November 1911.

He became a student of Lincoln Theological College under Michael Ramsey (later the Archbishop of Canterbury). In 1935, Chad became deacon of the new parish of St Giles in Lincoln, and was ordained as priest of the recently consecrated St Giles Church the following year.

His first task was to take the funeral of a teenager who had taken her own life through ignorance of the nature of puberty, and this led Chad to give public talks about sex.

He moved to London and in the 1950s founded the Samaritans. He was made an OBE in 1969 and Prebendary of St Paul's Cathedral in 1975.

RINGING OUT: STORIES OF BELLS

In the 1930s, there were more than 2,000 bells in Lincolnshire's churches. The largest in the county is Tom, the bell which chimes the hour at Lincoln Cathedral. Its diameter is 6ft 10.5in and it weighs 5 tons.

Crowland Abbey has the honour of being recorded as not only the first place in Lincolnshire where bells were rung, but also the first in England. Chronicler Ingulph recorded a seven-bell peal in the tenth century. The bells – called Guthlac, Bartholomew, Betelm, Turketyl, Tathyn, Pega and Bega – were housed in the central tower until 1091, when they were destroyed by fire.

The citizens of Lincoln knew that when Old Kate rang, it was curfew time. The bell, at the Church of St Benedict, was rung at 6 a.m. and 7 p.m. by John Middlebrook, whose house adjoined the bell tower. When he died, his job was passed to his widow, Mary, who found the task arduous as she grew older. So she came up with an ingenious idea; she made a hole in the wall between her bedroom and the bell chamber, and attached a rope to the bedhead, from where she could make Old Kate chime.

REDUCED TO RUBBLE... BY ACCIDENT

A Lincolnshire church was accidentally destroyed during the Civil War.

Troopers were drying gunpowder on Cornhill, in Lincoln, when it exploded. Embers spread, and some fell on the roof of St Swithin's Church.

A fire took hold, reducing the church to rubble. The ruin stood until 1718, when the south aisle was restored, and worship resumed until 1810, when a similar building was constructed, funded by industrialist Alfred Shuttleworth in memory of his father. It was designed by Louth architect James Fowler and the foundation stone was laid on Easter Day 1869 by the Bishop of Lincoln, Christopher Wordsworth.

St Swithin's is now Grade II-listed. A Roman altar was discovered during its second incarnation's construction.

THE PURITAN VICAR OF BOSTON

John Cotton led 300 Pilgrim Fathers across the Atlantic to Boston, Massachusetts, in 1630.

Seventeenth-century puritans felt they were being persecuted in England for their beliefs, so decided to leave the country to worship as they pleased.

A group of dissenters attempted to sail from Boston to the Netherlands in 1607 but were betrayed and promptly put on trial at Boston Guildhall.

The group were not thwarted, however, and later successfully sailed from Immingham in 1620. They became known as the Pilgrim Fathers, calling at Plymouth before making the voyage to Massachusetts aboard the *Mayflower*. Nine years later, the Massachusetts Bay Company was formed for people who planned to move there.

Cotton was Boston's vicar between 1612 and 1633, and lived at Tattershall Castle. He counted the 4th Earl of Lincoln and Theophilus Clinton-Fiennes among his many followers, and himself travelled to the US in 1633.

The first group to successfully flee from Boston did so in 1630, which included Lord Lincoln's steward, Thomas Dudley, and his daughter Anne Bradstreet.

Anne went on to become the first American poet to have work published. Her first known poem was entitled 'Upon A Fit of Sickness, Anno. 1632'.

There is a stained-glass window in St Botolph's Church, Boston, depicting nature lover Anne holding a bird's nest.

IMMORTALISED IN WORDS

A poem by Sir John Betjeman includes reference to 'an Indian Christian Priest', who is most likely to have been Asian Anglo-Catholic priest Theophilus Caleb, the vicar of Mareham-on-the-Hill who moved to Huttoft in 1943. An Asian priest was unusual for rural Lincolnshire at this time, but his devout spirituality endeared him to many. Sir John stayed with his friend Jack Yates in Louth and attended evensong in Huttoft, afterwards writing 'A Lincolnshire Church', containing the said line.

IMPORTANT RELIGIOUS FIGURES

Thomas de Aston: Born in about 1325, he studied at Oxford and Cambridge, and became a Bachelor of Common Law. He was ordained in the 1340s and was promoted to the Archdeaconry of Stow in 1386, meaning he had a permanent base in Lincolnshire. He is remembered for providing a chantry and almshouses for seven needy people in Spital-in-the-Street. He died in June 1401, and was buried in the nave of Lincoln Cathedral. His monument was destroyed in the Reformation.

George Boheme: A vicar of Sleaford but of Pomeranian origin, he was born in 1628. In August 1655, he was admitted to the living of Sleaford but ejected at the Restoration in 1660. During his time there, he had three children with wife Ann. Following his ejection, he lived in Walcot, several miles south of Sleaford, where he taught and preached in the village church, eventually being forbidden to do so because he was not episcopally ordained. Thomas Emlyn, the first Unitarian minister in England, was among his pupils.

Saint Guthlac: Of noble parentage, Saint Guthlac was a hermit who died at Crowland, a desolate island in the Lincolnshire Fens, in April 714. He spent several years engaged in warfare which he could not forget, and remorsefully joined Repton monastery in Derbyshire. After two years of penance, he copied the penance of the Desert Fathers and retired to Crowland. He spent fifteen years fasting daily until sundown and only then taking bread and water. Pilgrims would visit his cell, yet he was also subject to attacks. One of the pilgrims, Bishop Hedda, consecrated Guthlac's cell and raised him to the priesthood. During Holy Week in 714, Guthlac fell ill and announced he would die on the seventh day, which he did. Miracles were witnessed at his tomb, which became a focus of pilgrimage. He is said to have appeared after death to Ethelbald, predicting that Ethelbald would become king. This was realised in 716, and Ethelbald funded the construction of a large monastery. The hard work of the monks meant the fens of Crowland became one England's richest locations.

Alford is the birthplace of Anne Hutchinson, a figure in the history of the Pilgrim Fathers. She left with her husband and family to join John Cotton in America, and was commemorated in Boston with a bronze statue. She was the daughter of priest Francis Marbury, the master of Alford Grammar School, and in about 1612 married William Hutchinson, of Alford. Their eldest son, Edward, accompanied Cotton to Massachusetts and the couple joined them the following year. Anne admired Cotton's ministry and twice a week held meetings for women, but eventually differences arose and in August 1637, a synod at Boston condemned her. In November she was tried and banished, settling in Rhode Island in 1638 with her husband. In 1642, William died and Anne moved to New York County but she, her servants and all but one of her sixteen children – Edward – were murdered by Native Americans. Edward was murdered by Native Americans in 1673.

MORE INTERESTING LINCOLNSHIRE FACTS

Templar houses for the religious order of the Knights Templar were established in Lincolnshire. The best known is Temple Bruer, near Sleaford, where excavations in 1833 and 1907 revealed evidence of a Templar church with a typical circular nave. One of the towers was repaired in 1912.

There's an anonymous gravestone in the churchyard of St Peter's, Barton-upon-Humber. An unknown woman came to live in the town. She was at first accompanied by a man, who left after arranging accommodation. The lady died giving birth, and never revealed her name. The gentleman returned and took the child, and had the stone erected in 1777.

The 162ft-tall lead spire of St Mary's Church, Long Sutton, is believed to be the oldest such spire in England. It dates from the thirteenth century and was used as a sea-mark by mariners in The Wash for centuries.

Reverend George Watson, vicar of Caistor, would ride to surrounding villages to minister, and used the stables of a widow to house his steed. Rumours began to spread that they were having an affair, which so traumatised the vicar that he took his own life. He was cleared of wrongdoing by an inquiry and buried in the south aisle of Caistor's church.

Have you ever heard of a hudd?

Pinchbeck's church has one. It's similar to a sentry box, and was used by ministers to shelter from the elements while conducting burials. There are also hudds preserved at Donington, Quadring and Friskney.

CAUSING A STINK

When Lloyd George spoke at Louth Town Hall on 15 January 1910, he didn't expect this rather unusual reaction!

A male sympathiser of the suffragettes smuggled two women into the roof space, leaving them with provisions so they could stay there all day.

Before the politician uttered a word, the suffragettes dropped stink bombs through the ceiling grates. In the ensuing chaos, he was smuggled out through Cannon Street and down an alley that became known as Lloyd George's Passage.

A FIRST FOR ENGLAND

Louth MP Margaret Wintringham was the first Englishwoman to be elected to Parliament, the first female MP being American Mrs Astor.

She married Thomas Wintringham, of Little Grimsby Hall, in 1903 and became a headmistress in Grimsby. Mr Wintringham was the independent Liberal MP for Louth and when he died in 1921, his widow decided to stand for the by-election.

She won the seat – without once canvassing – and was defeated in October 1924. She was again unsuccessful in 1929 and 1935.

During the First World War, Mrs Wintringham served in the Voluntary Air Detachment and chaired the Women's War Agricultural Committee. After the conflict, she became a magistrate, sat on the Grimsby Education Committee and the Lincolnshire Agricultural Committee and represented Caistor with Lindsey County Council from 1933 to 1945.

She died in 1955, having proudly served Lincolnshire's interests.

BREAKING NEWS

On 27 May 1993, politician Norman Lamont resigned as Chancellor and from John Major's Cabinet – and the news was broken in a telephone call to his 82-year-old mother in Grimsby.

Irene Lamont promptly revealed the news – in a worldwide exclusive – to the *Grimsby Evening Telegraph*.

Mr Lamont had, for some time, been at the centre of growing concern about his future as Chancellor in Major's Conservative government, a position he had held for three years.

His mother prepared herself for an invasion of national newspaper reporters, but refused to speak to anyone but the local *Telegraph*. 'For the past three years they [the national media] have been at me and they have given Norman a very rough ride,' she explained.

Mr Lamont was born in the Shetland Islands and brought up in Grimsby, where his father was a surgeon. He studied at Cambridge and entered Parliament in the 1970s, serving in successive governments under Margaret Thatcher and John Major for fourteen years.

WHEN POLITICS CAUSED RIOTS

A fierce battle was being fought between Grimsby election candidates John Chapman and George Heneage in February 1862. It was in the days before the Reform Act, so every vote counted, and a rumour was circulating that Heneage was expecting two voters from Liverpool to boost his count.

On Election Day, 14 February, the out-voters were met at the railway station and taken to the nearby Yarborough Hotel. They were spotted by a local who told Chapman's supporters – by now fuelled with alcohol.

Chapman's men gathered outside the hotel, demanding that the pair show themselves. To calm the situation, landlord Mr Stephens allowed some inside.

Chapman's supporters returned to their friends and all seemed quiet – until the hotel was pelted with stones and a mob burst through the doors. At the time, Grimsby's police force had just eight officers.

Within an hour, almost everything inside was destroyed; the rioters attacked patrons, broke windows and threw furniture into the street.

Fortunately, there had been suspicions that Election Day would spell trouble, so between fifty and sixty officers from Hull were in town. The mob was removed and sixteen rioters were tried at the Lincolnshire Summer Assizes. Four were convicted of wounding, assaulting, beating and ill-treating their opponents and the police, and sentenced to three months' hard labour in Lincoln Prison.

The election was close run, with Chapman polling 458 votes and Heneage 446.

Years later, in April 1877, history repeated itself, this time when Liberal Alfred Watkin was elected as Grimsby's new MP following Chapman's death – but it was not a result everyone accepted.

Watkin provided transport for voters in outlying districts, whom some claimed had no business voting at all. He won, and went to the Yarborough Hotel to address a crowd of 1,000, who booed and shouted.

There had been much drinking, and stones were thrown through the hotel windows. A twenty-four-strong mob broke in. Inside, Watkin and his team were armed with stair rods, pokers, fire irons and a pair of pistols.

In the refreshment room, the gang drank 30 gallons of ale, a barrel of whiskey and half a barrel of port.

The police were outnumbered and a constable was knocked unconscious during the mayhem.

The Army was called, arriving the next morning to find the mob had vanished – leaving 200 broken windows and furniture reduced to scraps.

The hotel was repaired and a stone was put on display in the town hall as a reminder of a remarkable day.

10

THE SUPERNATURAL COUNTY

OLD JEFFREY: THE WESLEYS AND THEIR GHOST

In 1715, the Reverend Samuel Wesley and his wife Susanna experienced a haunting at their home, Epworth Rectory. They nicknamed the ghost Old Jeffrey, and several of the happenings were recorded in Samuel's diary.

The rectory has a turbulent history. On 9 February 1709 it was destroyed by a blaze and it was pure chance that someone saw a child standing at an upstairs window after the house had been evacuated and he was rescued by a human ladder. His mother, with astonishing foresight, described the little boy as a 'Brand plucked from the burning for a special destiny'; that little boy was John Wesley, the founder of Methodism.

A house was rebuilt on the site and it was here, between December 1715 and January 1716, where Old Jeffery haunted the attic. Eldest daughter Emily came up with the nickname because an old man by that name had died on the site previously.

The Wesley family, their friends and servants all claimed to hear the spirit knocking on the walls and floor of the attic. Often the noise of scattering coins could be heard, or breaking glass and the sound of chairs being thrown. Sometimes it sounded as if someone was planing wood. Doors in rooms would fly open and beds levitated.

Samuel recorded that the noises became more prolific when he said family prayers for King George. Despite advice, the family refused to leave the property.

TEN HAUNTED SPOTS

Digby Fen: In the 1900s, glowing lights were reported. They were believed to belong to a coach which had driven into a bog.

Gunthorpe: Commonpiece Lane is supposedly haunted by a white cat of abnormal size. Sightings were common among the locals for years. It is known that human bones lie buried nearby; farm labourers unearthed a skeleton while harvesting potatoes. The bones were reburied.

East Halton: The Manor House was apparently haunted by monks who had a religious house on the site. One set of inhabitants in the 1930s were so disturbed by the happenings that they put an iron pot in the cellar, laid the spirit in it, put pins and earth on top of the pot and left it there. Subsequent occupants were warned not to move it in case they disturbed the trapped entity.

Irby: In November 1455, Rosamund Avy (also known as Guy) and her fiancé Neville Randell were walking in woodland near Irby Top on the eve of their wedding. Villagers heard screams but the couple had vanished. Two years later, Randell returned to the village. He said that he and Rosamund had argued and he presumed that she had gone home. Some years later workmen unearthed bones at the spot.

Maidenwell: In Ostler's Lane, a spirit coach and horses goes by, and the coachman has his head in a box beside him.

Moortown: The road up to Moortown House was haunted by a big black dog that would vanish into the hedge at the same spot every time. A woman in a white apron was also often seen sitting in the hedge or walking along the road.

Morton, near Gainsborough: There is supposed to be a bottomless pit filled with water. At midnight, a lady in white rises and passes over the surrounding countryside.

Normanby: The valley stream between Normanby and Newton has a bridge over it. It was so haunted that three parsons were sent to lay the spirit, which would push people off the bridge. The parsons asked the spirit what it wanted. The spirit said it wanted a live stag, so while the spirit devoured it, the parsons trapped it in an iron pot.

Scremby: A headless bride is sometimes seen at midnight.

Sturton: The crossroads between Sturton and Scawby is known as Lidgett's Gap. Lidgett was a captain with Cromwell and lost his life during a battle with Royalists. He was buried under a big ash tree at the crossroads. People have seen a beggar haunting the spot, but it is unclear if this is supposed to be Lidgett. In the 1930s, the road was widened and human bones were discovered.

THE KNIGHT AND THE GREEN LADY

Sir John Bolle was the son of Charles Bolle, of Haugh, near Alford, and his family home was Bolle Hall, at Swineshead. In 1584, Sir John's uncle Richard built Thorpe Hall, at Louth, and the fortunate nephew inherited it.

Sir John married Elizabeth Waters, who stayed at Thorpe Hall while her husband travelled to Spain to serve his Queen.

He was involved in an expedition to Cadiz, during which he was responsible for looking after the welfare of its citizens. While the siege of Cadiz took place, a high-ranking Spanish lady, believed to be Donna Leonora Oveido, was taken prisoner. Sir John treated her with kindness and the lady fell in love with him.

She begged him to marry her, but not wishing to embarrass her, he said he had no money. She gave him all of her jewellery and £500, but he still declined, saying the crossing by sea to England would exhaust her.

Eventually he admitted he was already married, and the lady joined a nunnery, insisting he kept her gifts for his wife.

When they parted, she gave him a keepsake: a portrait of herself dressed in green, to take back to Thorpe Hall. He was knighted by Elizabeth I upon his return from Cadiz in 1596, and the portrait hung at the hall for 154 years after father-of-seven Sir John's death in 1606. Elizabeth survived him by forty-one years.

Soon, the Spanish lady's apparition began appearing at the hall. Dubbed the Green Lady, one of her favourite haunts is around the Five Sisters sycamore tree in the ground's deer park. A ballad was written about her, called 'The Spanish Lady's Love for an Englishman'.

It was tradition at Thorpe Hall for its inhabitants to lay an extra place at the dinner table, should the Green Lady wish to visit.

THREE CHEERS FOR HAUNTED PUBS

Black Horse, Eastgate, Lincoln: This hostelry is frequented by the Grey Lady, a well-dressed Victorian with a blurred face.

Green Dragon, Waterside North, Lincoln: An old woman, thought to be a previous occupant, has been spotted at the bar dressed in old-fashioned clothes and smoking a clay pipe. In the early 1950s, schoolboy Colin Hayes's father was landlord there. Legend said the pub was haunted by a spirit called Umbrella Mary, a woman who used to own an umbrella shop next door. Colin never gave the ghost a name; all he knew was that something would tug his hair as he went to bed every night.

The Centurion, North Hykeham: A regular spotted an elderly lady, dressed as if ready for bed. He turned to his friend to point her out, but she disappeared.

Ye Olde White Swan, Louth: This fourteenth-century pub is said to be haunted by an unusually tall ghost. He wears a white cape and patrols areas of the pub just before midnight.

TOAST TO A DEAD FRIEND

During the seventeenth century, notorious young gamblers Abraham Tegerdine, Mr Slater, Dr Jonathan Watson and Farmer Guymer met regularly at the Chequers Inn in Holbeach, near Spalding.

Guymer died and on the eve of his funeral his remaining friends met at their favourite watering hole to toast the memory of their chum.

Abraham suggested that the trio make their way to All Saints' Church nearby, to keep Guymer company.

They prised open the door and made their way to the altar, where they toasted their dead friend's body. Tegerdine suggested a game of cards, so they used the coffin lid as a table.

The game commenced but they were a man down, so Tegerdine suggested using Guymer's corpse as a dummy.

They opened the coffin, propped the dead man's body alongside them and commenced the game.

As they congratulated Guymer on his excellent card-playing skills, Guymer turned his head, leered at his friends and ordered three demons to whisk them away.

The townsfolk heard noises from within the church in the night but had been too scared to enter. At sunrise they discovered the upturned coffin, a scattered deck of cards, and Guymer's corpse propped up against the altar rail, grinning.

LONG TOM PATTISON AND THE DEAD HAND

In the seventeenth century, prior to the Lincolnshire wetlands being drained, locals were nervous of crossing them at night unless they carried a talisman or spells to protect them from the evil entities who lived there.

Long Tom Pattison would tease his friends for their superstitions, and eventually they challenged him to walk the path across the bogs.

A crowd gathered outside his mother's cottage on the appointed night. His mother tried to put something in his pocket, but Tom refused her talisman, picked up a lantern and made his way into the wetlands.

The onlookers went to bed, apart from some young ones who followed him. The chilly wind began to moan and ahead of them, Tom's lantern dulled. Tom shouted and swore in the dark, and was suddenly illuminated by a light.

The onlookers could see Tom's white face, his outstretched arm grasped by a disembodied hand. Known as the Dead Hand, it pulled him towards the bog and Tom, with a scream, vanished into the water.

The boys ran home and a search party was launched, but Tom was not found. In the following month, his mother went mad with grief and people avoided her. But one day she was spotted running along the bog path, asking for help. She led townsfolk to her son, who was sitting at the edge of the bog with his feet in the water, muttering gibberish.

Where he had been gripped by the Dead Hand was just a stump, and he was wizened like an old man. Tom never spoke again. He spent his days sitting alone and went into the wetlands at night. Within a year his mother was found dead, smiling contentedly. Her son lay dead in her lap, but his face was full of horror. Their fate was to haunt the wetlands for eternity.

BOSTON STUMP'S GHOSTLY FRIAR

St Botolph's Church in Boston is famous for its Stump; what's not so well-known is its ghost story.

A writer was entirely alone in the church, conducting research in the library, when he heard behind him the faintest of rustlings. He turned to see the tall figure of a Franciscan friar, who handed him the book he needed for his research.

The writer, convinced he had met a spirit, anonymously recorded the experience in a book called *Boston in Olden Times*, published in 1841.

TINKLING THE IVORIES

When darkness falls, a ghostly monk plays an organ at St Peter and St Paul's Church in Caistor. In 1967, the vicar tried to disprove the story by planting a cassette recorder in the locked-up church overnight. Organ music, footsteps and banging were all heard on the tape the following day.

HAUNTED LINCOLNSHIRE ROADS

A15: Near Ruskington, there are multiple records of sightings of a dark-haired man with pitted skin and an olive complexion, holding his left arm aloft. During the Second World War, a hermit who lived in the area was run over by an Army lorry. Further back in time, this spot was the scene of many highway robberies.

A16: Sightings date back to the 1950s of a glowing green mist coming from an old sandpit near Walmsgate and drifting across the road. Sometimes it takes on the shape of a man before dispersing. The pit became known as Green Man Pit.

Orgarth Hill, Louth: The spectre of an old man riding a shaggy horse has been reported since the 1860s.

A169 towards Grimsby: In 1985, a lady was driving as dawn broke when she saw a horse-drawn cart. She overtook it and looked in her rear view mirror to find it had disappeared.

ONE OF THE FIRST GHOSTBUSTERS

Robin Furman is known as Grimsby's ghostbuster.

The parapsychologist lives at Nuns Corner and saw his first ghost on the landing in his home there in the 1980s. He noticed movement and came face to face with a nun. She was wearing a habit and veil, and there was a glowing light where her face should have been.

During the reign of Henry II, the priory of St Leonard was sited at Nuns Corner. It was a poor priory and the nuns had to beg for support. It survived until 15 September 1539, when the last prioress, Margaret Riddlesdale, received a pension of £4 and other nuns were given annuities of 30s or 33s 4d.

Robin went on to establish one of the UK's first paranormal investigation teams, Ghostbusters UK.

A CRIMINAL'S DOG AND OTHER ANIMAL SPIRITS

The Strugglers Inn, in uphill Lincoln, is haunted by the ghost of a dog.

Poacher William Clark, from Norton Disney, was hanged in the nearby prison in 1887 for murdering a gamekeeper.

His faithful lurcher followed him everywhere, despite being subjected to cruelty and neglect by uncaring Clark.

When Clark was arrested, the dog would wander around the castle walls and scratch at the door of the inn. Unbeknown to the landlord, his wife felt sorry for the creature and fed it scraps of food.

At the very moment Clark was executed behind closed doors, the dog howled painfully... and then became a celebrity. The landlord welcomed the dog with open arms then, and many people came to visit.

The dog eventually died but the landlord, undeterred, had it stuffed and it was displayed on the bar for many years.

It's since been reported that the faithful dog's spirit haunts the inn.

Bolingbroke Castle is haunted by a hare, which is said to be the spirit of a witch who was held there. A phantom hare is also said to haunt the road between Kirton and Grayingham.

A sow and piglets appear at Halloween on Bonnewells Lane, Bransby, while the spirit of a large cat stalks Commonpiece Lane in Gunthorpe.

MONKS, A BLUE LADY AND A BOY...
ALL IN ONE HOUSE!

There are many ghost stories attached to Cadeby Hall, near Beesby.

The hall has had many owners and a rich history; in the late 1600s, for example, Hugh Hammersly, the vicar of Roxby, lost ownership of the hall to a member of the Pelham family during a game of cards. In 1986, it was listed as 'at risk' and was restored during the 2000s as a private home.

In 1885, George Nelson, a young boy, was thrown from his horse and died. A memorial stone marking the spot was erected, which now stands in a dyke bank on the A18. His ghost has been seen galloping nearby.

It is also believed that a boy's body was found in woodland close by the hall, and that the child's mother cursed the building and its inhabitants.

And if you're a guest at the hall, the last thing you want to see is a coach and horses on the drive – for it portends a death of a resident. It's said a phantom coachman will alight from the carriage and knock at the front door, disappearing before the door is answered.

DON'T STOP... IT MIGHT BE CLUBFOOT

RAF Binbrook opened in June 1940 for No. 1 Group, Bomber Command, and No. 12 and No. 142 Squadrons. No. 460 Royal Australian Air Force was also based there. On 3 July 1943, an electrical short circuit on a Lancaster caused its bomb load to drop onto the ground. The bombs exploded and the craft disintegrated.

A phantom airman has been seen at the end of the runway. It's believed to be the spirit of a sergeant who was part of the base's ground crew and in charge of loading bombers before take-off.

The station's most famous phantom is Clubfoot, an NCO armourer who was injured due to the carelessness of a pilot. He continued to work at RAF Binbrook but secretly plotted revenge. He tried to sabotage a Lancaster that the pilot was due to fly but as he fixed an explosive device, it exploded, killing him instead. Clubfoot's ghost is seen limping around the perimeter road of the base, trying to flag down passing vehicles.

THE SORROWFUL RED-HEADED AIRMAN

RAF Waltham was previously a private airfield and a training school for the Air Ministry, and during the Second World War it was home to No. 142 and No. 100 Squadrons. A total of 142 bombers were lost during this time.

In 1969, the Burchell family lived in a house built on the foundations of one of the station's Nissen huts. One of the family, Susan, awoke to find a one-armed red-haired airman standing in her bedroom. The figure moved towards the wardrobe and disappeared. It was said that the airman was declared unfit to fly due to injuries and, depressed, he killed himself inside the hut with a grenade.

On the eastern side of the former airfield is a memorial to No. 100 Squadron, where a spectral airman is seen standing at dusk.

THE BLACK LADY'S BROKEN HEART

Sightings of the Black Lady of Bradley Woods, near Grimsby, date from the 1920s.

The spectre of a pretty and pale young woman wearing a black hooded cape leaves witnesses with a feeling of sorrow.

Suggestions of her identity include a nun, a woman beaten to death by the father of her unborn baby during the First World War, and a spinster who once lived in the woods.

Another theory is that she is a woman who lived in the woods with her husband and son between 1455 and 1485. When her husband went to war, she would walk every day in the woods awaiting his return. One day, she was attacked by three soldiers who took her son. She spent the rest of her life wandering the woods and died of a broken heart.

MYSTERY OF THE ABANDONED HALL

Sometime during the reign of George VI, the family living at Harmston Hall, Waddington, abruptly abandoned it in the night and never returned.

Thirty years later, the hall was opened up for an inventory and the dining room was exactly as the family had left it. Chairs had been knocked over and there were wine glasses on the floor, with untouched wine still in the decanters. Locals said the squire had found out his wife was having an affair with his best friend. Rumour spread that the adulterous couple had been murdered and buried under the hearth.

Years later, a farmer took over the hall and became convinced that it was haunted. The family would hear screams, sounds of a struggle, running footsteps and the sound of a body falling against a door. In 1930, it became part of a mental health facility, which closed in 1990.

LINCOLN CATHEDRAL'S FAMOUS SPOOK

Robert Bloet (1094–1123) was the second Bishop of Lincoln. He was rather unpopular and was cursed by Roger the Hermit, a monk from St Alban's.

Bloet died from apoplexy while out riding with the King. His spirit apparently caused unpleasant incidents within the cathedral and it had to be exorcised. It is said his riding horn can still be heard within the cathedral walls.

REPORTED UFO SIGHTINGS

1953: A saucer-shaped object, accompanied by a humming noise, was seen in the sky above South Carlton, with two similar objects behind it. An orange light emitted from one of them. Two other parties reported seeing similar objects in the area at the same time.

1953: Ex-fighter pilot Neville Berryman, of Lincoln, saw a gold spherical object at 5,000ft travelling noiselessly at 1,500mph.

12 August 1954: A luminous white disc was spotted at 40,000ft above Gosberton, moving quickly and noiselessly.

12 December 1962: An unidentified object was spotted over RAF Coningsby.

1975: A bright white light passed over houses in Scunthorpe, causing blackouts in its shadow.

1976: A 45ft-wide triangular object was spotted travelling at between 15mph and 20mph 50ft above Ulceby Cross. There were two spotlights on the front of the craft and a bluish glow underneath.

October 1996: At three in the morning, police in Skegness witnessed a red and green rotating light over the coast. It remained stationary for four hours and could be seen by tankers out at sea and by the police in Boston. It was also traced by RAF Neatishead, in Norfolk, and on radar at RAF Waddington. There was still a radar trace of the object at 11 a.m. the following morning.

2000: A white object was spotted over Willingham Street, in Grimsby, while a silver cigar-shaped objected surrounded by a pink glow was seen in Waltham.

BIG CATS...

Sightings of big cats have been reported at the following locations:

Asterby
Baumber
Covenham
Dunholme
Gainsborough
Hartsholme Country Park
Hemingby
Holton-le-Clay
Kingerby
Lincoln
Ludford
Market Rasen
Normanby Cliff
Osgodby
Ruskington
Skellingthorpe
Stenigot
Tealby
Tetney
Walesby
Willingham Woods

...AND BLACK DOGS

Black dogs have been spotted around the county for years. There have been so many sightings that in the 1930s Lincolnshire folklorist Ethel Rudkin wrote a book about them.

Locations include: Blyborough; Leverton to Wrangle; Algarkirk; Bourne Wood; Moortown Hall; Brigg; Manton; Bransby; Gainsborough; Spalding; and Hemswell.

MONSTERS OF THE DEEP

A monster rising from the depths of the River Humber sparked a mystery in Grimsby.

Inshore boatmen, who earned a precarious living line fishing in the river, realised their lines were being stripped of fish. At first poachers were blamed, so early on 2 February 1934 two fishermen – Kirman and Reeder – kept a vigil.

Kirman, who had been standing up in the boat watching and waiting, gave a yell and fell back on Reeder. Speechless, he could only point at the water. The men saw a terrific swirl, rapidly moving away from the boat.

At a distance of 100 yards, a huge black shape broke the surface of the waves and, in a few seconds, disappeared as though diving, travelling in the direction of Tetney Haven.

Two days later, William Croft, who had spent fifty-one of his sixty years fishing, also saw the Humber Monster – and not for the first time. He'd seen it ten years before.

'You can take it from me it's no porpoise,' he said. 'It had a big head, like a Great Dane, ears and a mane on its neck. There was about two feet of head and neck out of the water.'

The first attempt to kill the creature proved almost lucky when a 'huge dark shape' was seen on a sandbank, but it was a tree trunk and, not missing an opportunity, was sawn up for logs.

Two days on, another armed squad set out but nothing was found... and mention of the monster was never made publicly again.

MORE SEA MONSTERS

The River Welland is home to a creature called Welly, said to be a plesiosaur.

In 1743, fisherman caught an 8ft-long beast in Fossdyke, which had webbed feet. In 1936, a monster with large eyes, long hair and walrus-like tusks was spotted in the River Trent.

At Trusthorpe in the late 1930s, holidaymakers saw a large serpent-like creature. Similar sightings were also reported off the Yorkshire coast at around the same time.

At Skegness in 1960 a dark-coloured creature was reported, and on 16 October 1966 a young couple were out walking when they saw a beast with six or seven humps, swimming at about 8mph at Chapel St Leonards.

THE WOLFMAN CANNIBAL

A wolfman lived on Read's Island in the 1800s. He was a traveller and would ferry people over the water for a fee, but while he lived there, people mysteriously disappeared. He was taken to court on a charge of cannibalism; the island was searched and hundreds of human bones were discovered. During his trial, the wolfman vomited and dropped onto all fours, howling. He was hanged for his crimes.

11

SPORT

FISH MERCHANT'S FIFA FIRST

Grimbarian Arthur Drewery was the first Englishman to become president of the international sporting body FIFA.

He was born on 25 March 1891 and educated at Grimsby Collegiate School. Aged 20, he joined the Lincolnshire Yeomanry, serving in Palestine and the Western Desert during the First World War and as head warden and chief fireguard in North Lincolnshire during the second.

He is well known for being a fish merchant from 1908 until retirement in 1953, and was also a JP and councillor for the town. But his name will always be synonymous with football. He was a director of Grimsby Town Football Club and president of the Football League from 1949 to 1955, as well as chairman of the English selectors for many years and taking on his role at FIFA.

Married to Ida, he was awarded a CBE in 1953 and died in Grimsby in March 1961.

WHAT A WINNER!
AND ANOTHER... AND ANOTHER...

William Elsley has the distinction of training 124 winning racehorses in 1905 – the greatest number of winners in one season by one trainer... until the record was broken by Henry Cecil in 1979.

William was born in 1855 at Hemingby, went on to marry Sarah Ann Scorer of Burwell in 1879, and the couple rented a 1,200-acre farm in Baumber to breed horses.

He turned a 60-acre field off Caistor High Street into a training ground and was soon winning; in 1898, his horse Lord Edward II won the National Produce Stakes at Sandown, worth £5,000. He employed seventy local men and his most successful jockey was Horncastle's Elijah Wheatley, who, in one year, rode eighty-three winners.

William, a father of five, was a trainer for thirty years and passed away in 1922.

NOW THAT'S CRICKET

When cricketer Martin Hawke became captain of Yorkshire in 1883 – a post he held for more than twenty-five years – he inspired his team to winning ways.

Born in 1860 the son of Reverend Edward Henry Julius Hawke, the rector of Willingham by Stow, Martin was privately educated and upon graduating from Cambridge was invited to play for Yorkshire, taking over the captaincy in 1883.

At the time there was a rule that only Yorkshiremen could play in the first team, but family connections with the county paved the way.

Yorkshire had never won the county championships but victory finally occurred in 1893; while Martin was captain, they went on to win another seven times, and he later led the England team in India, South Africa, West Indies, America and South America.

He stopped playing in 1910, becoming president of Yorkshire CC until his death in 1938, aged 78.

A FOOTBALL WIN...
THANKS TO JELLY BABIES!

In August 2014, a packet of Jelly Baby sweets helped Lincoln City FC win against league leaders Barnet.

Manager Gary Simpson told how the team bus failed to turn up for the match in London, meaning players had to make their own way there.

There was no room for the team's tactics board, so the boss used sweets in one of the kit lockers to demonstrate the team's formation. He praised the players' 'fantastic team spirit' in the circumstances and told the media that he would not rule out using Jelly Babies in the future.

'If we can keep winning I will do whatever is necessary,' he said. 'It wasn't the best situation to be in, especially when you are going to the league leaders that haven't conceded a goal, and had got off to an absolutely unbelievable start.' The match went 2:1 to Lincoln.

Simpson said the team often has Jelly Babies ahead of matches, but players usually eat them instead of using them as a substitute tactics board.

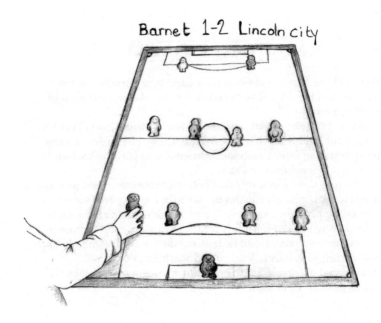

Barnet 1-2 Lincoln city

ONE OF THE BEST BRITISH GOLFERS

Tony Jacklin wanted a career in football, but when an ankle injury during a kick-about with friends prevented this, he went for a walk around Scunthorpe Golf Club instead – fast becoming a member and then achieving much sporting success, including winning twenty-four tournaments worldwide, such as the British Open in 1969, the US Open in 1970, the Italian Open in 1973, the Scandinavian Open in 1973 and the German Open in 1979. He also played in seven Ryder Cup matches and captained the European Ryder Cup team four times.

Tony was born in Bottesford in 1944. His first job was at Scunthorpe's steelworks and he later joined a local solicitors' firm, who let him have every afternoon off to practise golf.

Tony, who has twenty-seven tournament wins under his belt, appeared on *Strictly Come Dancing* in 2013.

RAYMOND'S FAITH IN GOOD LUCK CHARMS

During his thirty-year racing career, Raymond Mays never raced without wearing something blue.

He religiously carried good luck charms about him, including a small black cat and a black wooden doll, and he had a small ladybird sewn into his overalls.

The racing driver's charms must have done the trick, because just before the Second World War he broke many records on the old Brooklands circuit.

He was welcomed into the world on 1 August 1899, in Bourne; his father was a pioneering motorist, and mechanics from Vauxhall and Napier were always at his home because his father entered cars into hill and speed trials. A young Raymond persuaded the mechanics to let him sit with them during tests, and his addiction to racing was born.

In 1934, Raymond, Humphrey Cook and Peter Berthon formed English Racing Automobiles Ltd, and Raymond was number one driver. Raymond won the Nuffield Trophy race at Donnington Park, the first ever road race held in England, and so Raymond and his firm achieved fame.

He founded British Racing Motors (BRM) in 1945, embarking on a project to design an advanced racing car. It took a while but when Graham Hill qualified in one of the BRM cars and led the team to world championship in 1962, success was theirs. Later, Jackie Stewart joined. Raymond passed away in 1980.

FROM TEACHER TO PARALYMPIAN

Trainee teacher Jade Etherington, from Lincoln, became one of Great Britain's most successful female Winter Paralympians.

At the age of 23 Jade won four medals at the 2014 Winter Paralympics, part of a total of six for Paralympics Team GB.

The alpine skier, who has only 5 per cent vision in both eyes, has competed with her sighted guide, Caroline Powell, since August 2013. Alongside Caroline, she won silver in the women's downhill skiing, combined and slalom, and bronze medals in the Super-G at Sochi.

Jade and Caroline won three silver medals and a bronze at the 2014 Winter Paralympics, propelling them to claiming the title of the most successful British women Winter Paralympians ever. They were also the first Brits to win four medals during one Paralympic tournament. Jade proudly bore the British flag at the closing ceremony.

Jade revealed how she started to take sport seriously to cope with losing her sight at the age of 17. Born with glaucoma and Axenfeld syndrome, she paid tribute to her mum, who also has the condition, who started taking her on skiing holidays from the age of 8.

She had trials for the British Disabled Ski team's development squad, which distracted her from hospital appointments. She said: 'There is no point crying that you can't see any more. It is what you do to try to turn that into a positive.'

TEEN WENT ON TO GREAT THINGS

In the coastal village of Hogsthorpe, you will find the grave of an Olympian medallist.

Gladys Carson was born in Leicester in 1903. She and her siblings were good swimmers, and the trio became known as the Swimming Sisters.

Gladys' sporting career began when she was small. Such was her natural talent that, aged 18, she won the breaststroke championship of All England with a time of 3 minutes 12.4 seconds.

Her prowess ensured her a place in the Olympic team. Aged 21, she was funded by the British Olympic Association to travel to Paris to compete in the 1924 Olympics, which featured in the 1981 film *Chariots of Fire*.

In Paris, Gladys was advised on everything from how to behave on the train to how to get to the Folies Bergère!

On 18 July 1924, Gladys competed in the finals of the women's 200m breaststroke, coming third with a time of 3 minutes 35.4 seconds, winning the bronze medal for Britain.

She passed away in November 1987 and was buried in Hogsthorpe.

A WORLD CHAMP IN GRIMSBY

Snooker player Ray Edmonds was born in Grimsby on 25 April 1936. He is a former professional English billiards and snooker player, and twice won the World Amateur Snooker title.

Not only that, he won the World Professional Billiards Championship in 1985, putting Grimsby firmly on the sporting map.

Ray's career first took off as an amateur, taking the World Amateur title twice in the early 1970s. He then went professional, and reached the World Snooker Championship four times – in 1980, 1981, 1985 and 1986. Each time, he lost in the first round.

In 1985 though, Ray won the World Professional Billiards Championship, giving him the unique distinction of being the only player to have won that title as well as two World Amateur titles at snooker.

During this time, he established the Ray Edmonds Snooker Centre in Grimsby in December 1983. He also worked for ITV and the BBC as a snooker commentator before retiring in 2004.

FROM STRONG CHILD TO STRONGMAN

Strongman Geoff Capes showed sporting prowess from the start, when he won 7s 6d in an under-9s race while wearing Wellington boots.

Born in 1949 in Holbeach, Geoff played soccer for the Lincolnshire Schools XI and basketball for Holbeach, and took up weightlifting when a club was set up in his hometown.

At the age of 17 he showed his strength when a wheel came off his van, and he lifted it up with one hand to replace the wheel with the other!

After school, the strapping lad – who was over 6ft tall – worked with his father on the land and once loaded 20 tons of potatoes in twenty minutes.

In 1969, he joined the police, becoming a PE instructor, and left the force just before the Moscow Olympics in 1976.

In 1974, he set new Commonwealth and British throwing records, and later competed in the Highland Games and TV strongman contests.

Geoff was three times Britain's Strongest Man, three times European Strongest Man and two times World's Strongest Man.

If that wasn't enough, he also won the World Highland Games five times!

WHEN SHANKS TOOK OVER THE REINS

Bill Shankly is among the well-known sports personalities to have served Grimsby Town FC in its time.

He was appointed as manager of the club on 6 June 1951, and stayed for more than two years before resigning on New Year's Eve 1953.

Shankly, affectionately known as Shanks, joined the Mariners from Carlisle, and had nearly done so a year before as coach, but the Carlisle board improved his contract.

In his first season at Blundell Park, Grimsby Town won eleven games in a row – a club record – but just missed promotion.

Shanks took over the reins at Workington in 1954 after earlier saying, 'At one time I had visions of staying at Grimsby for the rest of my life, but that's football. Things change a lot.'

While Shankly failed to lead Town to promotion, the next-but-one manager, Allenby Chilton, hit the spot.

He came from Manchester United to become the Mariners' first player-manager, and so successful was the team that they became the first club in Football League history to go from re-election one season to promotion the next.

SOME MORE SPORTING STORIES

Karen Corr spent her teenage years in Bourne, and began playing snooker and billiards aged 14. She turned professional in 1990 and during her career participated in the Ladies' World Championships eight times. In 1991, she reached the semi-final of the World Mixed Doubles with partner Jimmy White, and in 1993 she raised almost £2,000 for charity by playing in a continuous twenty-eight-hour snookerthon. She was given the freedom of Bourne in 1991 in recognition of her achievements.

In 1929, professional endurance swimmer Miss Mercedes Gleitze visited Skegness to swim the Wash to Hunstanton. She made several unsuccessful attempts from Skegness, instead finally resorting to making the shorter crossing from Butterwick in thirteen hours and seventeen minutes. Mercedes was the first person to swim the Straits of Gibraltar and the first British woman to swim the English Channel.

Skegness-born international goalkeeper Ray Clemence was awarded an MBE in 1987. He was educated at Lumley Secondary School, and went on to become keeper for Liverpool and Tottenham Hotspur. He was capped sixty-one times for England, and later became keeping coach for England.

Well-known Derbyshire cricket player William Cropper, a forward with Staveley FC, died in the changing room at Grimsby Town's ground. It was January 1889, and during a game between the teams Cropper was accidentally kneed in the stomach by Grimsby fullback Daniel Doyle. Cropper made it clear he blamed no one for the accident and it was thought he had only suffered minor injuries. But his health rapidly deteriorated and he spent the night in the dressing room, where he died the following day.

Jackie Beeton raced motorcycles from 1931 to 1964, and was British Champion in 1958. He worked with his father, William, at the family garage in Upgate, Louth. Les Nutt was Jackie's sidecar passenger and they raced internationally, as well as on their home patch, Louth's famous Cadwell Park circuit. When Jackie was away racing, the garage was run by his father and Jackie's son, Peter. Peter worked there from 1960 to 1994, when it closed. Peter also raced – in motocross – and later went into classic car restoration.

The late Sir Denis Follows – who organised the 1966 World Cup – was born in Lincoln in 1908. He had a flair for organisation and was secretary of the Council of the Football Association between 1962 and 1973. When he retired from the FA, he became treasurer for the Central Council for Physical Recreation and then chairman of the British Olympics Association. He received a CBE for organising the World Cup and was knighted in 1978.

HE SHOULD HAVE BEEN A STONEMASON...

Grimsby-born Freddie Frith won the Senior TT race on the Isle of Man in 1937, with an average speed of 88.21mph.

Frederick Lee Frith OBE – known as Freddie – was a popular man in and around his home town. Born in May 1909, he trained as a stonemason but declined to join the family business – a firm of funeral directors in Scartho – to ride instead.

He won the 1935 Junior Manx Grand Prix and then joined the Norton team for the 1936 TT, where he claimed the Junior TT title and finished second in the Senior TT, as well as winning the 350cc European Championship.

In fact, he was five times the winner of the Isle of Man TT, and had the distinction of being one of the few to win TT races before and after the war; in 1937, he set the first 90mph lap of the Snaefell Mountain course.

Freddie also had the honour of being the first ever 350cc World Champion in 1949, when he won all five events of the inaugural campaign.

During the Second World War, he served in the Army at the Infantry Driving & Maintenance School stationed at Keswick. There Sergeant Frith taught officers how to ride cross-country in all weathers.

Many people will have visited his motorcycle shop in Victoria Street, Grimsby, which stocked classy Italian bikes. He retired to St Mary's Park, Louth, where he died in 1988.

ROYALTY OF THE WAVES

Grimbarian Brenda Fisher successfully swam the English Channel in 1951, becoming a world record breaker in the process.

Brenda was born in 1927, the daughter of a skipper, and learned to swim aged 9. She found she had a talent for speed swimming, but developed an interest in distance swimming, under the tutorship of Herbert McNally.

In August 1951, she became the 23rd swimmer of the English Channel from France to England, completing in a record women's time of twelve hours and forty-two minutes – seventy-three minutes faster than the previous women's record set by Jenny James. She won the first prize – £1,000 from the *Daily Mail*.

She swam the Channel again in 1954, and was again the first woman ashore. Two years later, she won the 29-mile River Nile swim in the fastest recorded time, followed by the 32-mile Lake Ontario swim. This epic journey, from Niagara to Toronto, took Brenda eighteen hours and fifty minutes, enduring a thunderstorm as she swam. She beat the record held by Marilyn Bell by two hours and six minutes – only the third person in history to complete the swim.

Brenda, who was married to Grimsby Town player Pat Johnson, retired from competitive swimming aged 31 and became a swimming teacher.

Brenda's wasn't the area's first success in the Channel. On 22 August 1935, Haydn Taylor also conquered the waves.

Born in Sheffield, he became a dentist in Cleethorpes. He set off from Cap Grisnez, near Calais, at 1.35 a.m. and arrived just west of Dover at 4.23 p.m.

The crossing, of fourteen hours and forty-eight minutes, was, at the time, the eighth fastest ever recorded. Taylor was also the first man to swim the River Humber. A keen athlete, he served with the City Battalion in the First World War and was wounded on the first day of the Battle of the Somme. He died in 1962.

SHIRLEY: WHAT A BLOOMING STAR

Shirley Bloomer – the British, Italian and French hard courts champion, Britain's number one and a Wightman Cup veteran at the tender age of 23 – brought sporting fame to Grimsby.

She was born on 13 June 1934 and at the age of 12 won the Lincolnshire 18-and-under Girl's Tennis Championship.

She won three Grand Slam titles during her career, and was the second ranked singles player in the country in 1957.

Her many sporting successes include being crowned the French Open Champion in 1957, the number one woman in Europe, world number three and British number one.

She competed in the Wimbledon Singles an impressive nineteen times between 1952 and 1974.

In 1959 Shirley married Chris Brasher, who helped Roger Bannister run the first sub-four-minute mile in 1954. They had three children, including their daughter Kate, who played on the women's professional tennis tour in the 1980s.

12

THE WEATHER

WHEN HELL CAME TO LOUTH

It is known in Louth as Black Saturday, and described as one of the worst disasters England has known.

The 29 May 1920 was a dark day in more than one sense; gas lamps had to be lit in most houses from 2 p.m. Without warning, a vicious thunderstorm caused a waterspout to descend from the sky in the Wolds west of Louth, prompting exceptionally heavy rain.

The rain swept through Hubbards Hills towards Louth, converging at Westgate Road Bridge, where debris quickly built up. The debris formed a dam, the bridge partially collapsed and a torrent of water rushed along the River Lud, into the heart of the town, causing a flood of devastating proportions.

The river normally flows peacefully at 16ft, but it was transformed into a raging body of water, sweeping along everything in its path – including animals, cars, trees, carts and even a summerhouse, which was moved 50 yards.

The volume of water was so large that a tar-sprayer, weighing 1.5 tons, was lifted over a mass of debris, and the stone bridge spanning Bridge Street simply crumbled. The gap this left behind saw 7.5 million tons of water pass through it.

A firefighter at Louth Borough Fire Station was killed when water damaged the building, and three houses and their occupants were washed away in Ramsgate. A resident described the water as flowing like a high wall, then collapsing like a pack of cards. Entire streets were under water.

The water sped on to Ramsgate Road railway bridge, onto a large, low area of land and the grounds of the Priory. At the time, the Priory was home to the Mayor, Councillor Lacey. His house was flooded and he lost much furniture. His wife was at home at the time, and rescued twenty-four sheep grazing on the Priory field by pulling on waders and herding them to higher ground.

The water continued to spread throughout Eastgate and Ramsgate Road, entering Hall's Mill Dam and flooding buildings until reaching an unused canal basin. Gradually the water went into Marsh Drains, and out into the North Sea.

Miraculous tales of escape emerged. One pedestrian saved himself by clinging to a lamppost for several hours. A butcher saved his wife and children by climbing onto the roof of their home and staying there for four hours.

Dr Willie Higgins was attending a woman in labour when the flood struck. The bottom half of the house was submerged and water soon crept upstairs, within a foot of the mattress on which the patient lay. The woman's husband reacted quickly by jumping out of the bedroom window into the torrent – which was 13ft deep – to get help, but he could not swim. The doctor swam to the man, noticed a floating ladder and got them back to the bedroom safely, where his patient gave birth to a daughter.

Using the same ladder, he got the new mother and baby to hospital, and then returned to save five children, working through the night to bring them to safety. When he got home, wet and exhausted, to his house in Bridge Street, it had been devastated by the water.

An inquest heard how a paralysed woman could not make it upstairs, and her devoted daughter refused to leave her. They died in the flood together. In all, twenty-three people lost their lives.

After the water subsided, the streets were thick with silt. A recovery operation was supported by the King and Prime Minister, and the Mayor of Louth opened a relief fund, raising £90,000 from donations, including £16,000 from the *Daily Mail* newspaper.

Today, a memorial stands in Louth cemetery and flood markers can still be seen around the town.

STRANDED BY THE SNOW

High winds and 20ft snowdrifts caused so much havoc in the Wolds in February 1947, that food was dropped off to cut-off villages by plane.

Work was disrupted, schools closed, buses and cars were left abandoned and thousands of people were unable to leave their homes… conditions were so severe that snow ploughs were rendered useless for ten days, and coal lorries could not make deliveries.

Mrs Irene Trevor, of the Marquis of Granby Inn at Binbrook, told the *Lincolnshire Chronicle* how they had no beer and were looking after twenty-seven passengers from stranded buses bound for Grimsby, who had nowhere to go. She told the newspaper that there were 'people sleeping in every room, even in the bar'.

Meanwhile, Great Limber's postman, Mr R. May, valiantly struggled against the elements on horseback to deliver mail.

Mr H. Smith, head shepherd at Lodge Farm, in Normanby-le-Wold, reported a strange occurrence. He was digging out sheep from drifts and when the animals were brought into the open, blocks of ice as big as footballs quickly formed around their heads due to condensation. Crows and magpies, spying an opportunity, landed on the defenceless sheeps' backs and began pecking at them. The sheep were then wrapped in sacking for protection.

1953: WHEN THE EAST COAST WAS RAVAGED

In January 1953, the Lincolnshire coast flooded; the biggest peacetime tragedy the country has ever seen.

Some 307 lives were lost and 24,000 homes damaged or destroyed, and days later, more than 1,000 people remained untraced along the battered, flooded coastline.

Lashed by winds of hurricane force, the North Sea ripped gaps in the sea defences.

From Grimsby and Cleethorpes in the north to Canvey Island in the south, roads turned into rivers and the sea smashed through homes and businesses along the entire east coast.

Peter Blanchard was a projectionist at the Ritz Cinema, in Grimsby Road, Cleethorpes, and was working when the waves hit. He recalled going up on the roof with a friend, the wind so strong that they had to cling onto each other.

'We could see water coming along Grimsby Road towards the cinema,' he said. 'The chief projectionist, Sid Melhuish, had gone home earlier because his house backed onto the railway. When the sea broke the embankment, it smashed through the back and front walls of his house. We could see straight through the house to what was left of the embankment with the railway tracks hanging across the gap and nothing inside the house. A lot of other houses had similar damage. All that had happened at the Ritz was the organ pit had flooded.'

MORE WICKED WEATHER: LINCOLNSHIRE'S WILD SIDE

A freak tornado up to 100ft high swept down the Humber in August 2000. The giant twister sucked up water from the river as it swirled in a northerly direction for about fifteen minutes, narrowly missing land. The Humber Coastguard kept an eye on the natural phenomenon, which was dying down and resurfacing on a regular basis as it made its way along the coast. The tornado was the culmination of bizarre weather conditions affecting the area, which included ferocious hailstorms, prolonged thunder and lightning strikes, and thick fog – all within a twenty-four-hour period.

In January 1905 a tidal wave, prompted by a gale, wrecked a section of the sea wall at Cleethorpes. The repairs cost £26,430, and used 13 tons of shingle, 1,600 of cement, 5,600 of chalk, 4,432 yards of concrete slabs, 12,900ft of kerb and channel, 7,000 piles and 6 miles of planking.

In February 2008 at about 1 a.m., Grimsby residents had a rude awakening – they were shaken from their sleep by the worst earthquake to hit the UK in twenty-four years. While most homes escaped relatively unscathed, some buildings had to undergo twelve months of structural repairs. Its epicentre was several miles away in the Lincolnshire village of Market Rasen, and the quake measured 5.2 on the Richter scale. Chicken farmer Peter Sargent kept his poultry one field away. He said, 'I went into the shed as normal and there, in one corner, were seventy-two dead birds without a mark on them. I am convinced they flocked to one corner when the ground shook and died of suffocation and fright.'

Flood warnings came too late to save the Lincolnshire coast in January 1976 from its worst night in years. Huge waves sent water and mud pouring through hundreds of properties. Met Office warnings were flashed to police headquarters just half an hour before the sea began pouring over coastal defences. Within an hour, houses were engulfed in miniature tidal waves and the Grimsby-Cleethorpes railway line was washed away.

In January 1987, ambulances were taking emergency cases only as cold weather brought on a spate of heart attacks. Grimsby was virtually isolated as driving snow cut off major and minor routes; a siege-like situation which lasted a few days. Ambulance workers slept in their stations and had to be dug out to attend casualties. Not only were there sudden heart attacks, but a myriad of broken bones from people slipping in the icy conditions. Tragically, one woman died and another man, aged in his early 40s, collapsed and died outside Scartho Road swimming baths. A 62 year old died at the wheel of his car while attempting to start it. One motorist had to dig himself out three times in the space of 80 yards and eventually gave up; another, George Smith, was stranded for thirteen hours after setting off for work. Milk supplies and morning paper deliveries were disrupted, lorries jack-knifed and there were miles-long tailbacks on clearer roads. A special incident room was set up by the police to deal with weather-related incidents and panic-buying set in as worried families feared running out of food.

WHEN THE ELEMENTS STRIKE BACK:
TRAGEDIES AND LUCKY ESCAPES

In May 1962, a 13-year-old girl had a miraculous escape when lightning struck her home.

Ann Patricia Fruen was sitting in the living room having her lunch when there was a flash of lightning, a clap of thunder and smoke poured from the television set. The aerial was flung into the garden of a neighbour and Ann's dress was singed.

Decorations completed when the family had moved into the house about three months previously were damaged. Other homes were also struck by lightning; television and radio sets were damaged, and telephone lines put out of action.

Sixty ships on the coast between Grimsby and New Holland were wrecked during a high tide on 6 October 1571. It was not the first, or the last, time the Lincolnshire coast felt the effects of flooding; there are references to such natural disasters as early as 1178. The 1571 flood devastated the low-lying land. It was caused by two factors – heavy rainfall over the whole of the south of England, swelling all the main rivers, and a storm surge down the North Sea. It was the onshore wind which led to the multitude of shipwrecks, and huge numbers of livestock were drowned. Records say 20,000 cattle and at least 3,000 sheep were lost on the North Sea coast alone.

Just outside Grimsby, shepherd Spencer and his flock of 1,800 sheep drowned when the sea burst through the walls, constructed of earth, along the shoreline.

Hollingshead's 'Account of Damage Done In The County of Lincoln, by The Tempest of Wind and Rain' records that the village of Mumby Chapel (north of where Chapel St Leonards is now) survived, but with just three houses. A ship smashed into one of the homes, and the mariners climbed onto the roof, saving a mother they found there. Her husband and child perished.

Skegness men Richard West, Samuel Moody and John Moody were given cash rewards for the courage they displayed during a storm in 1825. The Finnish vessel *Maria* was in danger of being blown ashore, so a rescue boat was deployed and fired lines at the ship, saving eleven men. Two men tragically drowned as they tried to reach the beach in another boat.

A violent thunderstorm claimed the life of 12-year-old Arthur Ryan, from Boston, in 1899.

When he failed to return home after a trip out on his own, his brother went looking for him. He was found by the side of the road in Middle Drove. Lightning had struck him on the head, passing through his body and burning out through his left knee. The strike had burnt his trousers and split open his left boot. Underneath him was an open-clasp knife, which Arthur had been using when the lightning struck.

During the same storm, two men were hurt and a horse was killed by lightning in Sutterton. Drover John Green was carrying a pint of beer in Booth's Passage, off Norfolk Street, when lightning struck the pitcher. He was left with just the handle in his hand.

Back in September 1844, 300 Bostonians turned out alongside the fire brigade to extinguish a large wheat stack which had been struck by lightning. Despite their best efforts, nature won out and the stack was destroyed.

The pleasure boat *Shannon* left Skegness for a routine trip into The Wash, under a clear, bright July sky in 1893. Suddenly dark clouds gathered and a gale-force wind began to whip the vessel. On land at Skegness, rain had turned into a torrential downpour, causing rivers. Cousins Edward and Edwin Grunnill were at the helm of the *Shannon*, struggling to keep her afloat. Without warning, the mast snapped and the canvas collapsed, capsizing the *Shannon* in seconds. Jabez Grunnill was in a nearby fishing boat and was almost wrecked himself, but the storm subsided as suddenly as it began and Jabez rescued three people. Twenty-eight people perished, including the cousins in charge and day-trippers from London. For days afterwards, bodies were washed ashore. A national disaster fund for dependents raised more than £6,000.

FIVE CHURCHES SUBMERGED BY STORMS

St Peter's, Mablethorpe (1276)   Sutton-in-the-Marsh (1571)
Skegness (1526)   Mumby-cum-Chapel (1571)
Trusthorpe (1571)

WHERE TO WATCH A TIDAL WAVE

At the time of the spring and autumn equinoxes, a tidal wave travels along the River Trent. It is known as the Aegir, the name given to it by Scandinavian settlers whose river god was called Oegir. The natural phenomena is mentioned in George Eliot's novel, *The Mill on the Floss*. A good place to watch the tidal wave is at Morton, near Gainsborough.

WATERY PREMONITIONS

In June 1971 the submarine HMS *Artemis* was in Grimsby, waiting to sail the following day.

Grimsby woman Sandra MacDonald made friends with some of the sailors. The week after *Artemis* sailed, Sandra had a dream.

'I saw a big grey wall – I thought it was a harbour – and I saw the submarine sink,' she recalled. 'In the dream, three men were trapped on board.' She told her mother about the nightmare, who reassured her. But a week later, on 1 July, the sub actually did sink – and three men were trapped on board, two of them Sandra's friends.

'It frightened me,' she said. 'I'd heard about premonitions but I was sceptical about it.' The story was featured on the TV programme *Arthur C. Clarke's World of Strange Powers*.

When she sank, *Artemis* was in just 9m of water while moored at the HMS *Dolphin* shore establishment at Gosport, refuelling. She was raised five days later, decommissioned and sold for scrap.

In 1805, John Clarke from West Butterwick went to West Stockwith Fair but failed to return home.

At the time, a brig was moored at Kelfield and its captain had a vivid dream that a man was robbed, thrown in the river and that the body became caught up on a moored boat.

The captain awoke and went outside to find Mr Clarke's body snared up in the cable of his own boat. Two men were arrested but no further action was taken.

13

ON THIS DAY IN LINCOLNSHIRE

5 January 1945: Beachcomber Marshall Haley discovered the 'Mablethorpe Find', a haul of bronze Roman coins in an earthenware bowl. The coins were dated by the British Museum as from varying reigns of emperors, from Augustus in 27 BC to Constantinus in AD 361. It wasn't Marshall's only success in discovery; in 1935, he found the remains of an Anglo-Saxon village in Mablethorpe.

15 January 1943: Lincoln endured its worst air raid of the Second World War. A lone Dornier dropped incendiary and phosphorous bombs, killing four people and wounding thirty. A bomb dropped in Thomas Street exploded two days later and destroyed seventeen homes.

26 January 1899: Skegness's first motor car made its debut. It was purchased by garage owner Bill Berry, Lion Hotel landlord Freddy Kirkby, Whale Museum owner Joe Wingate and Richard Lloyd to provide tourist rides. Their journey from London to Lincolnshire to bring home the Daimler – which had a top speed of 12mph – took three and a half days.

31 January 1934: The New Waltham Wireless Station's wooden mast caught fire 300ft up and burned for forty-eight hours. The station opened in 1907 by the coastguard and was taken over by the Royal Navy in 1910. For two years after the fire, the station operated with two temporary masts, which were replaced in 1936 by five metal towers used during the Second World War. The towers were toppled in August 1980.

2 February 1829: Robbers targeted Halstead Hall, near Stixwould, bursting in on Mr and Mrs William Elsey as they dined and threatening them with a gun. The couple and their maid were tied up by the men, who stole property and money. Labourer Thomas Lister was caught and confessed to being at the hall, but said no more. He was hanged on 27 March. Thomas Strong and Timothy Brammer were executed in 1830, while Richard Poucher was transported in 1831.

15 February 1901: The steamship *Homer* was in collision with a Russian barque, 20 miles off the River Humber mouth. *Homer* was sailing between London and Newcastle, while the Russian ship headed for America. The foreign crew survived, and all but one seaman, McAllister, perished on the *Homer*. Its wreck lies in 26ft of water; one of an estimated fifty in the river mouth.

1 March 1848: The first public railway service in the Grimsby area began operating. It ran between Louth, on the East Lincolnshire Railway, and New Holland on the Manchester, Sheffield and Lincolnshire Railway.

13 March 1928: A Stinson aircraft, *Endeavour*, took off from RAF Cranwell in wintry conditions. Experienced fighter pilot Captain W.G.R. Hinchcliffe, who fought in the First World War, was at the controls. His co-pilot was a 34-year-old socialite, the Honourable Elsie Mackay, who wanted to be the first woman to fly the Atlantic. *Endeavour* was last seen on radar 400 miles west of Cranwell, at County Cork, before it vanished.

26 March 1881: Skegness fisherman Henry Moody had a lucky escape when his shrimping cart became entangled with the wreck of a Spanish vessel that had sunk forty years previously. Mr Moody was caught out by a fast-moving tide. He cut free his horse and left the cart to the waves.

27 March 1907: At 10 p.m. a train laden with Grimsby fish travelling to Lincoln collided with a derailed goods train from New Holland. The incident, at Brocklesby Junction, saw both engines land on their sides, and the wagons were smashed to pieces. The fish had been packed by Grimsby merchants Sam Chapman & Sons in time for Good Friday – traditionally a big selling day for fish.

5 April 1942: Wrens Yvonne Lillian Capon and K. Wainwright inadvertently found themselves in a minefield in Seacroft Road, Skegness. A mine detonated, killing Yvonne. Her friend lost a foot and suffered facial injuries. They lay undiscovered until passers-by Thomas Jennings Malone and his wife heard cries. Thomas died in an explosion as he tried to reach the women. His wife suffered minor injuries.

7 April 1681: The Great Fire of Caistor was sparked in the home of John Sheriffe, and within three or four hours, houses, barns, stables, shops, warehouses and more were destroyed. There were fatalities, and forty-five families became homeless. Damage worth £6,786 was caused.

14 April 1892: A whale swam into the River Humber and became stranded just inside Spurn Point. The creature died but, realising it could be exploited for cash, the carcass was towed to Cleethorpes and exhibited during the Easter holidays. As per custom, the whale was claimed on behalf of the Crown by the Receiver of Wrecks, which ordered its sale. The highest bidder was Matthew Dowse, a Cleethorpes refreshment rooms proprietor, who paid £75. The skeleton was later put on public display.

22 April 1939: Skegness had two football teams – Skegness United and Skegness Blue Rovers. On this day, they met for the last time in the final of the Skegness Nursing Cup. The Blues won 2–1. The clubs never reformed after the war.

30 April 1831: The wooden floor of the privy at the Bull Inn in Bottesford covered a vault 3 yards deep, and was in a notoriously bad state of repair. Four children went inside and were dancing when the floor gave way. The youngsters – including the daughter of the pub's landlord – all suffocated.

15 May 1912: Electric single-decker trams began operating between Grimsby and Immingham, mostly used by the docks' workforce. The last tram service ran on 1 July 1961.

17 May 1817: Heckington grazier Samuel Jessup died at the age of 65. It was later discovered that, in the last twenty-one years of his life, he had taken a staggering 226,934 pills, supplied by a Bottesford apothecary. He also owned 40,000 bottles of mixtures.

26 May 1973: The Wash from Skegness to Hunstanton was conquered for the first time by Sutton-in-Ashfield journalist Kevin Murphy, in thirteen hours and fifty-four minutes. He had previously swum the English Channel and the Irish Sea.

31 May 1898: An inquest was held into the death of a man who had jumped off the Albert Bridge into the River Welland, at Stamford. Moments before, a newspaper boy had handed him a sheet of paper. The man placed it in his pocket and jumped. The inquest heard how the man, Mr Thompson, believed people were after him all over town. A piece of paper was found on his body containing sketches of saucepans and indecipherable writing.

10 June 1821: A storm of hail, thunder, lightning and rain was so severe that the afternoon service at Carlby's church was postponed. A good job too, for a 'ball of fire', presumably a lightning strike, caused an explosion in the steeple, setting the rafters alight. The lead melted and a wall collapsed in the empty church.

12 June: This date is known as John Dalderby Day. Day was born in Horncastle and became Bishop of Lincoln in 1300. When he died, miracles were attributed to him, including restoring speech to the people of Rutland, who could only bark. A service is held each year in Lincoln Cathedral.

19 June 1215: The Magna Carta was signed in Runnymede, Surrey; Lincoln Cathedral holds one of just four remaining copies. The Magna Carta was a charter of liberties between King John and rebel barons. The Charter of the Forest – providing rights for the common man – was issued in November 1217. Two copies remain, in Lincoln and Durham's cathedrals. This charter was in force until 1971.

21 June 1936: The German airship *Hindenburg* was spotted over Lincoln on a training flight. It was capable of carrying seventy people at a time, and made more than sixty flights, mostly to America. It caught fire in 1937, and many passengers died. In mid-1939, following reconstruction, it was kitted out with wireless equipment for the Luftwaffe, and made the world's first ever electronic surveillance flights over Lincolnshire. The airship's sister, *Graf Zeppelin II*, was fitted with electronic equipment and in 1938 flew along the east coast, including over Mablethorpe and Cleethorpes, to uncover the secrets of British radars.

3 July 1938: The A4 pacific loco *Mallard* reached the highest speed ever recorded by steam locomotive in the world. The London and North-Eastern Railway began a series of high-speed trials on the line between Grantham and Peterborough. The *Mallard* achieved 75mph at Stoke, 100mph at Corby Glen and 120mph at Little Bytham, peaking at 126mph.

28 July 1937: Harold Davidson, a former rector, died after being mauled by a lion while performing with Fred Rye's Lions at Skegness's Pleasureland amusement park.

29 July 1831: Richard Codling and Thomas Motley were executed at Lincoln for their part in the Swing Riots, an uprising of agricultural labourers over poor wages and other issues. Incidents in Lincolnshire included arson attacks on stacks at Alford, Easton, South Reston, Swaby, Spalding, Spilsby and Stickford. Codling and Motley set fire to a shed containing farming equipment and oat straw, belonging to Lusby farmer John Cherry.

1 August 1645: Robert Jermyn's mansion on the banks of the Trent at Torksey was burned down during a skirmish. It had been seized by Parliamentarians in September 1644, and raiding Royalists from Newark Castle destroyed it.

23 August 1873: A train excursion from Lincoln to Skegness prompted a swarm of complaints from residents. It was reported that the raucous visitors – both male and female – decided to bathe nude on the beach 'to shock the modesty of the natives' and visitors.

24 August 1911: Lincoln city firefighter Alfred Clay and his crew were called to a blaze at the four-storey Osbourne's Motor Works. A crowd gathered on the banks of the River Witham, hooting and cheering when a shortage of water made the fire engine slow down. Bricks and stones were thrown at a constable as he struggled in 3ft of water to move the hose. After the fire was damped down, there was a stampede as Alfred Clay tried to keep the crowd away from an unstable wall. The wall collapsed on him and tradesman Mr T.H. Starmer. They were pulled from the wreckage but Mr Clay did not survive.

1 September 1939: The evacuation of Grimsby schoolchildren began. They assembled outside their schools, the first leaving from Hilda Street, Weelsby Street and Holme Hill, who were sent to Alford. Harold Street School pupils were destined for Horncastle; Little Coates pupils for Sutton-on-Sea and Mablethorpe; Spilsby was the destination for those from Victoria Street, Strand Street and St Mary's; and Woodhall Spa welcomed pupils from St John's.

7 September 1809: You'd have been forgiven for doing a double take if you saw this peculiar sight. For a bet, a waiter trundled a hoop from Sleaford to Lincoln – without once letting it fall or touch his body.

14 September 1296: Gilbert of Lafford, rector of St Peter's Church, Normanby-le-Wold, was assaulted during evening service on Holy Cross Day. A group described as 'sons of Belial' stirred up by a 'diabolical spirit' rushed inside and attacked the rector and his clerk, causing serious injuries. The perpetrators were excommunicated in every neighbouring church.

1 October: This date has been officially celebrated as Lincolnshire Day since 2006, marking the anniversary of the Lincolnshire Rising in 1536, when Catholics revolted against the Church of England.

11 October 1913: This day marks the only time a complete peal rang at Boston's Stump in the giant chamber before it was modernised. The chamber was in such bad condition that even in daytime, ringers worked by candlelight. Bells were hung so low that a tall man could touch them, which meant the noise was terrific. A peal of Stedman Triples – of 5,040 changes – was rung in three hours and twenty-one minutes by eight members of the Lincoln Diocesan Guild of Church Ringers, conducted by Reverend Law James. The team tried fifteen times before success.

7 November 1564: A fish measuring 6 yards between the eyes and with a 15ft-broad tail was caught in Lincolnshire. It was so big that twelve men could stand upright between its jaws.

13 November 1912: Skegness's lifeboat carried out one of its most famous rescues. Heavy seas stranded the Norwegian cargo ship *Azha* on Skegness Middle Sands. Its eight-man crew were rescued, and lifeboat coxswain Matthew Grunnill and second-cox Montague Grunnill where awarded medals of courage by the King of Norway.

17 November 1849: At his shop in Eastgate, Louth, chemist William Armitage attempted to invent a detonating signal for use on the railways in fog. He put a number of the devices to dry in an oven when they exploded. William, his father and three other people were killed, and the building burned to the ground.

13 December 1286: Overnight, a great flood affected the east coast from Lincolnshire to Essex. The church of St Peter's, in Mablethorpe, was destroyed. There was another flood on 13 January 1287 that claimed many lives, and another the following year on 4 February 1288.

16 December 1943: An RAF attack on Berlin became known as Black Thursday, when twenty-five Lancasters were lost and others crashed on their way home in fog. Overall, 483 Lancasters and ten Mosquito bombers took part in the attack, including seventeen Lancasters from 100 Squadron and fifteen from 550 Squadron, both based at RAF Waltham, near Grimsby. As the crews neared the airfield on their return, visibility was poor. At 11 p.m., Lancaster HW-H crashed at Ratcliffe Top, less than 4 miles from home. The pilot and three crewmembers perished, and three injured. Around the same time, 100 Squadron commander David Halford crashed while trying to land at RAF Kelstern. He and four crewmembers were killed. Two were thrown clear of the explosion but badly injured. At 11.19 p.m., the first Lancaster successfully landed at RAF Waltham, while others continued circling. At 12.40 a.m. on 17 December, two 100 Squadron Lancasters crashed in fog over Waithe. One of the aircraft hit the ground on fire and six crewmembers died, but a resident bravely rescued rear gunner Sergeant Wallace. Tragically, he died in hospital in January 1944. The other aircraft fell near Grainsby Church and all crew perished.

BIBLIOGRAPHY

Anderson, C.L., *Lincolnshire Links with Australia 1788–1840*,
  C.L. Anderson, 1988
Barley, M.W., *Lincolnshire and the Fens*, Batsford, 1952
Binnall, Peter, *The Nineteenth Century Stained Glass in Lincoln Minster*,
  Friends of Lincoln Cathedral, 1966
Brandon, David, *Haunted Lincoln*, The History Press, 2009
Bray, Christopher, *The Enemy in Our Midst*, KM Associates Ltd, 1987
Cawkwell, Norman, *Louth & About from Edwardian Times*, Norman
  Cawkwell, 2009
Cawkwell, Norman and Harrison, John, *More Louth & About*, Norman
  Cawkwell, 2009
Chapman, Peter, *Images of North Lincolnshire*, Breedon, Books, 1993
Codd, Daniel, *Mysterious Lincolnshire*, DB Publishing, 2013
Crust, Linda, *Ration Books and Rabbit Pie: Lincolnshire Folk Remember the
  War*, Society for Lincolnshire History & Archaeology, 2008
Cuppleditch, David, *Around Louth in Old Photographs*, Sutton Publishing, 1989
—, *Around Louth: A Second Selection*, The History Press, 2003
—, *A Century of Grimsby*, The History Press, 2007
—, *The Lincolnshire Wolds*, Budding Books, 2001
Cuppleditch, John R., *Lincolnshire Women*, self-published, 1998
Day, Jason, *Haunted Grimsby*, The History Press, 2011
Felix, Richard, *The Ghost Tour of Great Britain: Lincolnshire*, Breedon
  Books, 2006
Fisk, Roy, *Historic Lincoln*, Roy Fisk, 1986
—, *Lincoln Scrapbook: Peeps into the Past*, 1989
—, *Reflecting Lincolnshire*, 1983
Gordon, Kaye, *Gayton-le-Marsh & Tothill: A History*, self-published, 2006
Gray, Adrian, *Hidden Lincolnshire*, Countryside Books, 1994
—, *Crime and Criminals in Victorian Lincolnshire*, 1993
—, *Lincolnshire Headlines*, Countryside Books, 1993
—, *Tales of Old Lincolnshire*, Countryside Books, 2011
Green, Herbert, *Forgotten Lincoln*, Lincolnshire Publishing Co., 1897
Hall, Geoff and Fears, Doug, *The Dummy Airfield K Site*, self-published, 1996

Hanson, Martin and Waterfield, James, *Boston Windmills*, 1991

Hardy, Clive, *Grimsby at War*, Archive Publications in association with the Grimsby Evening Telegraph, 1989

Horan, Chris, *Humber Sail and History*, Chris Horan, 2010

Howat, Polly, *Ghosts and Legends of Lincolnshire and the Fen Country*, Countryside Books, 1999

Hurt, Fred, *Lincoln During the War*, self-published, 1991

Jones, Michael J. and Rooke, Peter, *Lincoln: Townscapes Through Time*, Cottage Publications, 2010

Kaye, David, *Wolds' Lore*, Horncastle Bus Club, (undated)

—, *Shire County Guide: Lincolnshire*, Shire Publications, 1995

Kazimierczuk, Elaine, *A Lincolnshire Notebook*, Hutton Press Ltd, 1991

Ketteringham, John R., *Lincolnshire Natives and Others*, John R. Ketteringham, 2002

—, *Lincolnshire People*, The King's England Press, 1995

—, *A Second Lincolnshire Hotchpotch*, The King's England Press, 1990

Kightly, Dr Charles, *Churches of the Western Wolds*, 1991

King, Sarah and Hillery, Caroline, *Lincolnshire Discovery Guide*, Discovery Group of Publishing & Marketing Companie, 1998

Kime, Winston, *The Lincolnshire Seaside*, The History Press, 2005

—, *The Skegness Date Book 1850–2000*, Skegness Town Council, 2006

King, P.K. and Hewins, D.R., *The Railways around Grimsby, Cleethorpes Immingham & North-East Lincolnshire*, Foxline Publishing, 1998

Large, John, *Stories from the Fens and the Wolds*, John Large, 2001

Leach, Terence R., and Pacey, Robert, *Lost Lincolnshire Country Houses*, Old Chapel Lane Books, 1990

Leith, Mary, *What Happened to Joe?*, Workers' Educational Association, 1995

Lund, Brian, *A Lincolnshire Childhood*, Reflections of a Bygone Age, 2011

Morsley, Clifford, *News from the English Countryside 1851–1950*, Harrap, 1983

Naylor, Stanley, *Lincolnshire Country Life Beside the Wash*, Stanley Naylor, 2000

Noble, James, *Around the Coast with Buffalo Bill: The Wild West in Yorkshire and Lincolnshire*, Hutton Press Ltd, 1999

O'Neill, Susanna, *Folklore of Lincolnshire*, The History Press, 2012

Pateman, John, *Lincolnshire Asylums*, lulu.com, 2012

Peasgood, David, *Grimsby: A History and Celebration*, Francis Frith, 2012

Rands, Eric, *More Memories of a Marsh Village: Portraits of Immingham*, Immingham WEA, 1970

Richards, Steve, *Grand Old Ladies*, Archive Publications, 1990

Robinson, David N., *The Book of Louth*, Barracuda Books, 1979

Rudkin, Ethel H., *Lincolnshire Folklore*, EP Publishing, 1987

Russell, Rex C., *From Cockfighting to Chapel Building*, Heritage Trust of Lincolnshire, 2002

Stennett, Alan, *Lost Railways of Lincolnshire*, Countryside Books, 2007

Sizer, Stuart and Chambers, Peter, *A Mablethorpe Trail*, self-published, 1990

Skinner, Julia, *Did You Know? Lincolnshire: A Miscellany*, Francis Frith, 2010

Smith, Martin, *Stamford Myths & Legends*, Paul Watkins, 1991

Start, David, *Lincolnshire From The Air*, The King's England Press, 1993

Start, David and Hall, Collette, *Lincolnshire's Heritage*, Heritage Trust of Lincolnshire, 1996

Stennett, Alan, *Nobbut A Yellerbelly!*, Countryside Books, 2006

Storey, Neil R., *A Grim Almanac of Lincolnshire*, The History Press, 2011

Sutton, Maureen, *A Lincolnshire Calendar*, Paul Watkins, 1997

Thompson, Albert E., *Skegness Pier 1881–1978*, Albert E. Thompson, 1989

Tierney, Janet, *Grimsby In Old Photographs*, Sutton Publishing, 1990

True North Books, *Memories of Lincoln*, True North Books Ltd, 2013

Wade, Stephen, *Hanged at Lincoln*, The History Press, 2009

—, *The A–Z of Curious Lincolnshire*, The History Press, 2010

Washbourn, Peter and Pat, *Lincolnshire: The Way We Were*, Breedon Books, 2001

Wilkinson, Marjorie C., *Skegness at War*, self-published, 2008

Wood, Lucy, *Blonde in Deep Water: Brenda Fisher: The Story of a Channel Swimmer*, Kindle Edition, 2016

—, *The Grimsby Book of Days*, The History Press, 2014

NEWSPAPERS AND MAGAZINES

Grimsby Telegraph

Lincolnshire Echo

Lincolnshire Life

Lincolnshire Past & Present

Jabez Good's Lincolnshire Glossary

WEBSITES

www.britishnewspaperarchive.co.uk

www.lincstothepast.com

OTHER

Lincolnshire Archives

Skegness Pier 1881–1971, Souvenir Issue

Also from The History Press

𝔐ediaeval 𝔐ystery

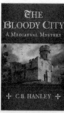

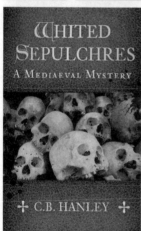

A gripping murder mystery series set in
a time of violent civil war and featuring
commoner-turned-earl's-man, Edwin Weaver